HENRY C. ELLIS

The University of New Mexico

THE TRANSFER
OF LEARNING

The Macmillan Company, New York
Collier-Macmillan Limited, London

Library of Congress catalog card number: 65–15182

THE MACMILLAN COMPANY, NEW YORK
COLLIER–MACMILLAN CANADA, LTD., TORONTO, ONTARIO

Printed in the United States of America

Fourth Printing, 1969

Foreword

"The Critical Issues in Psychology Series," new paperback source books for the undergraduate in psychology, are designed to provide authoritative and provocative reviews of selected topics germane to a spectrum of courses. Each volume offers an original inquiry into major facets of the point at issue and a set of illuminating reports carefully chosen to represent salient positions of historical or current significance. This combination will afford instructor and student opportunity to read stimulating, even challenging, argument with primary sources in hand.

The extent to which the learning of one task affects the subsequent learning of other tasks is, obviously, a matter of prime importance to all of us. Educators have long recognized the practical implications of this problem of transfer of learning; psychologists have similarly recognized its theoretical significance. This volume offers a thorough review of transfer from both points of view and includes the treatment of historical as well as contemporary contributions.

Henry C. Ellis, author of *The Transfer of Learning*, has concentrated on this problem in his research program and has had consistent federal grant support. He has been especially interested in problems of stimulus predifferentiation as a contributor to the net transfer effects. Since receiving his doctorate at Washington University in 1958, Professor Ellis has been on the staff at The University of New Mexico.

MELVIN H. MARX, *General Editor*

Preface

LONG SIGNIFICANT IN THE PSYCHOLOGY OF LEARNING AND in educational psychology, the findings, theories, and problems of the transfer of learning, are provided easy access within this volume. A special effort has been made to underline the major results of research and to suggest new perspectives in reviewing current problems.

The early chapters are concerned with the nature and measurement of transfer, followed by several chapters devoted primarily to summarizing empirical findings. Emphasis has been placed on both the older more traditional topics in transfer as well as some of the new problem areas such as mediation and stimulus predifferentiation. Subsequently, the reader is introduced to some of the problems involved in applying principles of transfer to educational settings. Both laboratory and classroom studies are viewed as complementary and some discussion of their relationship is given. Finally, a survey of some of the more active developments in theory is presented. Part Two contains articles on transfer that illustrate or document significant points and provide opportunity to read the original literature. Hopefully, this may offer a basis for more detailed consideration of the issues.

My thanks go to Professors Allan G. Barclay, M. E. Bunch, Slater E. Newman, Sidney Rosenblum, and James M. Vanderplas, who critically read several chapters of an early draft, and to Professors Arthur R. Jensen and J. L. Buyers, who read a draft of Chapter VII. Above all, I am extremely grateful to Professor Melvin H. Marx, general editor of this series, for many thoughtful suggestions and useful criticisms. Miss Susan Sharpe and Mrs. Eleanor Orth were responsible for a very accurate typing job, and my wife Florence contributed toward the clarification of obscure points and checked the references.

HENRY C. ELLIS

Contents

PART TWO: The Selected Readings

PART ONE

Inquiry and Argument

CHAPTER I

The Nature of Transfer

AMERICAN VISITORS TO ENGLAND OCCASIONALLY REPORT that they experience difficulty in driving on the left side of the street because of their established habit of driving on the right. What happens in some instances is the tendency to revert momentarily to driving on the right or to vacillate between right and left, even though the rules of driving in England are clearly understood. In a similar vein, a common experience of individuals who begin to drive a car with an automatic transmission, after having driven only cars with standard transmission, is to attempt to depress a nonexistent clutch pedal. In both these situations we see that earlier learned habits, or modes of responding, can affect performance on some subsequent task that in a general way describes transfer of learning.

Transfer of learning means that experience or performance on one task influences performance on some subsequent task. Transfer of learning may take three different forms: (1) performance on one task may *aid* or facilitate performance on a second task, which represents *positive transfer;* (2) performance on one task may *inhibit* or disrupt performance on a second task, which represents *negative transfer;* and (3) finally, there may be *no effect* of one task on another, in which case we have an instance of *zero transfer.* Zero transfer can occur either as a result of no effect of one task on another, or as a result of equal effects of positive and negative transfer that cancel.

Casual thought confirms numerous instances of transfer, both negative and positive, which occur daily. An instance of positive transfer is seen when, having learned to drive the family car, one finds it relatively easy to drive the next-door-neighbor's car (providing, of course, they have the same type of transmission!). Similarly, students who have thoroughly mastered the principles of algebra find it easier to grasp advanced work in mathematics such as calculus. The influence of transfer is pervasive and is found not only in intellectual tasks and in complex motor skills but is seen in emotional reactions and attitudes of individuals.

FORMAL DEFINITION OF TRANSFER

Although transfer of learning has been described in a general way, it is best understood in terms of the way it is usually measured. As shown below, the simplest type of study of transfer requires both an experimental group and a control group. The experimental group learns some initial task, Task A, and then learns a second task, Task B. The control group does not learn Task A, but does learn Task B. If there is positive transfer from the learning of A to B, then the experimental group should perform better (for example, learn faster) on Task B than the control group.

Experimental Group:	Learn Task A	Learn Task B
Control Group:	—	Learn Task B

On the other hand, if the experimental group is inferior in performance on Task B, as compared with the control group, we conclude that negative transfer has occurred. In this case, we conclude that the learning of Task A in some way inhibits or interferes with the learning of Task B. Finally, if the experimental and control groups perform the same we have zero transfer. It is assumed that the experimental and control groups are equivalent with respect to factors important in learning the tasks, for example, intelligence, and that during the interval in which the experimental group learns Task A, the control group either does nothing during this period or practices some *unrelated* task. What the control group does during this period is crucial in the interpretation of transfer; this will be made clear in Chapter II.

SIGNIFICANCE OF TRANSFER

There is perhaps no more important topic in the psychology of learning than transfer of learning. Some, such as Deese (1958) flatly conclude that there is no more important topic. From a very early period in life, much new learning is probably influenced in some fashion by previous learning. For example, the response that young children make when entering a new school may be influenced by their previous experiences with school environments; similarly, the response of a college student to a particular course may be affected by his previous experience with similar courses and with the kinds of expectations he may have acquired. It is difficult to think of any adult learning that could not be affected by earlier learning. We might, in fact, regard all studies of learning beyond a very early age as studies of transfer of learning.

Many educational and training programs are based upon the assumption that what is taught in the classroom or in the training program will transfer to new situations. Students are sometimes taught arithmetic with the hope that what is taught will be useful in a variety of daily activities such as making change and balancing the checkbook. Similarly, industrial employees are placed in training programs on the assumption that what they learn will carry over into the daily activities of the job. For example, pilots are taught complex discriminations using simulated cockpits on the assumption that these discriminations, such as learning to read the altimeter correctly, will carry over to the actual flying task. In view of the fact that many educational and training programs are designed to teach for transfer, it is important that psychologists discover the conditions that govern transfer of learning.

The problem of the psychologist working on the topic of transfer of learning is at least twofold: (1) to determine the fundamental conditions or variables which influence transfer of learning, and (2) to develop a comprehensive theory that will integrate and unify the knowledge about these variables. In turn, a significant task facing the educational psychologist and training specialist is to assist in the design of curricula and training programs based upon existing systematic knowledge of transfer. Their task can be conceived as one of maximizing the conditions for positive transfer and minimizing the conditions for negative transfer.

BRIEF OVERVIEW OF TRANSFER RESEARCH

Historically, early research on transfer was aimed at determining the gross effects of practice with one task upon another, answering questions about teaching methods, examining theoretical issues such as the doctrine of formal discipline (Thorndike and Woodworth, 1901), which contends that the mind can be trained and made more disciplined by studying certain subjects, and making inferences about brain physiology by way of bilateral transfer studies (Woodworth, 1938). Examples of these early investigations are studies to investigate the transfer effects of learning Latin to other subject matter (Pond, 1938) and the transfer effect of memory training (Woodrow, 1927).

Unfortunately, many early studies of transfer failed to specify the precise variables producing transfer, even though positive or negative transfer may have been obtained. In other words, a transfer effect was obtained but the specific variables producing the effect could not be easily determined in all instances; this type of experiment has been called *nonanalytic* by Underwood (1957).

To illustrate a nonanalytic experiment, suppose that one wishes to investigate the effects of a type of teaching method on the ability of students to solve mathematics problems. One group of students is taught using this special teaching method, and they receive additional homework problems as well. Another group, presumably a control, is taught in a traditional way without the extra homework problems and with a different teacher. At the end of the experiment, the students are tested on various problems, and it is found that the group trained with the special method performs significantly better in solving problems than does the control group. Unfortunately, one *cannot* conclude that it is the special teaching method that leads to improved performance in solving problems because the groups differed in at least two other ways: (1) in the amount of homework they had and (2) different teachers. Either or both of these factors could have produced the difference in problem solving between the two groups of students. In short, a nonanalytic experiment is one in which a difference occurs, but one is not sure *why* the difference occurred.

In recent years there has been increased emphasis on more analytic approaches in transfer designs. The studies of Bunch (1936), McGeoch and his associates (1931), and McKinney (1933) serve to mark the beginning of this trend, and the classic paper of Melton (1936) aided in the standardization of research methods in human learning and transfer.

A chief effort of these more analytic studies of transfer was their attempt to analyze the fundamental *dimensions* of transfer tasks. Transfer tasks can vary with respect to many dimensions, such as the degree of similarity between the tasks, which can be further analyzed into both stimulus similarity and response similarity, variety of tasks, and complexity of tasks, just to mention a few. By analyzing the variety of task variables in a more detailed or molecular fashion it became increasingly possible to specify what precise factor or factors produced transfer. Examples of this shift in emphasis toward a more analytic approach in transfer research can be seen in more recent studies (for example, Gibson, 1941, Osgood, 1946, Porter and Duncan, 1953, Postman, 1962, Young and Underwood, 1954, Vanderplas and Garvin, 1959). In summary, contemporary research in transfer of training is generally aimed at determining *why* transfer occurs—that is, discovering the exact variables that influence transfer, whereas earlier investigations were more concerned with whether transfer did occur.

CURRENT ISSUES AND PROBLEMS IN TRANSFER

Current issues and problems in transfer of learning can be conveniently classified in four major areas: (1) those which deal with the research methodology and the more technical problems associated with the measurement of transfer; (2) the specification of the major variables influencing transfer of learning and the *way* in which these variables influence transfer; (3) the development of adequate conceptual models or theoretical structures for organizing our knowledge about transfer; and (4) the development of an educational technology which is capable of translating and applying our knowledge of transfer to the great variety of educational and training problems that exist.

In the first area, a question of considerable importance is: "What are effective ways of measuring transfer of learning?" In the second area, concern is with the various experimental conditions or factors which influence transfer. A typical question representative of problems of this type might be: "Should one practice a great deal on one task or less with several similar tasks in order to maximize transfer?" The third area concerns the developing of a theory of transfer, and a typical question might be: "Is this particular theory of transfer valid for certain kinds of learning?" Finally, the fourth area concerns itself with more practical problems of attempting to apply knowledge about transfer to educational and training situations. A frequently asked question is: "How can we organize the school curricula so as to best ensure positive transfer?" In other words, "How can we teach for transfer?"

This book will discuss all four of these problem areas. We will first deal briefly with some problems in the measurement of transfer. Then we will consider the role of various factors in influencing transfer of learning and examine some of the theoretical conceptions of transfer that have been developed. Finally, we will attempt to apply our knowledge of transfer principles to various practical problems in education and training.

CHAPTER II

The Measurement of Transfer

THIS CHAPTER DESCRIBES SEVERAL TYPES OF DESIGNS and formulas used in transfer studies. It is important to note that the findings of different transfer studies can depend easily upon the way in which transfer was measured. In addition, if we wish to compare the results of several studies that use different kinds of tasks or measure performance at different stages, we need to know something about transfer formulas. Excellent discussions of the measurement of transfer can be found in several sources (for example, Andreas, 1960, Gagné, Foster, and Crowley, 1948, Murdock, 1957, Osgood, 1953, Woodworth and Schlosberg, 1954).

TRANSFER DESIGNS

A summary of the more frequently used transfer designs is shown in Table 1. Design 1 has already been described in Chapter 1. With this design, an experimental group learns Task A followed by Task B, and a control group learns only Task B. This is a frequently used design, but suffers from a major weakness. A number of experiments have shown that the learning of a task can be facilitated by an immediately preceding activity (for example, Hamilton, 1950, Thune, 1950) and by previous practice on a number of similar tasks (Harlow [3] [1]). These effects are, respectively, warm-up and learn-

[1] Bracketed numbers refer to readings in Part Two.

ing to learn. More will be said about these effects subsequently; for the moment, they are briefly noted for purposes of understanding certain problems in transfer designs. If an experimental group does perform better than the control group on the transfer task, we are not sure if the superior performance is due entirely to the specific features of Task A or due to the more general effects of warm-up or learning to learn. Transfer may, of course, be due to the summation of all three of these effects. Because Design 1 does not control for possible warm-up or learning to learn, it is not a desirable design if one wishes to know the *specific* effects of Task A as distinguished from the *general* factors described above. If there is no need to isolate these effects, then the design is acceptable.

Design 2 is one in which the subjects are tested on a portion of Task B, designated as B^1, prior to their assignment to either the experimental or control group. This method is the fore-and-after-test method described by Woodworth and Schlosberg (1954). Such a procedure has the advantage of matching the two groups on their performance on B^1 so that their equivalence prior to the experiment is assured, provided that the experimenter assigns subjects to the groups on the basis of performance on B^1. In addition, if sufficient practice on B^1 is given, then the groups are more likely to be equal in possible warm-up effects. Unfortunately, since the experimental group still receives more practice (it practices on Task A), differences in performance on Task B itself may still be a function of differences in learning to learn this type of material.

Design 3 is one in which half the subjects learn A followed by B and half the subjects learn the reverse sequence. This type of design has been used in studies of inter-sensory transfer—that is, transfer from one sensory system to another (Lifton & Goss, 1962). One problem encountered with this design is the necessity of assuming that practice effects from A to B are the same as from B to A.

Design 4 requires that the subjects in the experimental group learn Task A and then Task B; subjects in the control group learn Task A and then a similar but not identical task, B_1. This design keeps the original task the same and introduces variations in the transfer task. It has the important advantage of controlling the factors of warm-up and learning to learn, so that differences in performance on the transfer task can be attributed to specific features of the task itself. The chief difficulty is ensuring that Tasks B and B_1 are themselves equivalent—that is, equally difficult to learn in the absence of Task A learning. If B and B_1 are not equivalent in difficulty, then we cannot be sure that differences in performance on Tasks B and B_1 are due to transfer effects themselves, or due to differences in inherent difficulty between the tasks. In general, it is necessary to know if Tasks B and B_1 are equally difficult prior to using this design. Examples of this type of design can be seen in the work of Gibson (1941) and Hamilton (1943).

TABLE 1

Summary of Several Transfer Designs

Design	Group		Original Task	Transfer Task
1	Experimental		Learn A	Learn B
	Control		(Rests)	Learn B
2	Experimental	Pretest on B^1	Learn A	Learn B
	Control	Pretest on B^1	(Rests)	Learn B
3	Experimental		Learn A	Learn B
	Control		Learn B	Learn A
4	Experimental		Learn A	Learn B_1
	Control		Learn A	Learn B
5	Experimental and Control		Learn A	Learn B

Design 5 requires that all subjects learn Task A and then Task B with different intervals of time elapsing between the two tasks. This design has been used extensively in studying the temporal course of transfer (Bunch and McCraven, 1938, Ellis and Burnstein, 1960). Groups learning at different time intervals may serve as controls for each other. In addition, control groups based on performance on Task B alone may also be used.

TRANSFER FORMULAS

The amount and direction (positive or negative) of transfer is usually determined by employing one of several transfer formulas. The three transfer formulas described below are similar in that they involve making comparisons between the experimental and control groups on performance on the transfer task.

In order to apply a transfer formula to a given set of data, some measure of performance must have been taken. Measures frequently used include: (1) the number of trials required to reach a given level of mastery; (2) the amount of time required to reach a given level of mastery; (3) the level of mastery reached after a given amount of time or number of trials, such as the number of correct responses; and (4) the number of errors made in reaching a given criterion of mastery.

A simple transfer formula is described below. Let E represent the mean performance of the experimental group on the transfer task (Task B) and let C represent the mean performance of the control group on the transfer task (Task B). By comparing the difference between E and C groups with C itself a percentage transfer formula can be expressed as follows:

$$\text{Percentage of transfer} = \frac{E - C}{C} \times 100 \qquad (1a)$$

This formula is appropriate if the measure of performance is such that the *larger* the value of the measure, the *better* the performance. For example, if the measure of performance is the number of correct responses, then the formula is appropriate because the number of correct responses becomes larger with better performance.

Formula (1a) will be illustrated with a simple example. Suppose we conduct a transfer experiment in which we measure the effect of taking French this year on the taking of German next year. In other words, we want to know if taking French will aid or interfere in the subsequent learning of German. We employ two groups: an experimental group that studies French for a year and then takes German the following year and a control group that studies only German. In this instance, Design 1 is employed. A measure of performance is taken on the first test on German and we discover that the E group averages ninety correct responses whereas the C group averages only seventy-five correct responses on the test. Applying Formula (1a) and substituting the values for E and C, we obtain:

$$\frac{90 - 75}{75} \times 100 = \frac{15}{75} \times 100 = 20 \text{ per cent transfer}$$

The E group shows 20 per cent transfer, which means that the E

group performs 20 per cent better in German compared with the C group. Of course, we do not know if the positive transfer is a result of the specific features of French or of learning to learn; it is likely a mixture of both.

Formula (1a) must be modified by reversing the numerator to $C - E$ if the measure of performance is such that the smaller the value of the measure, the better the performance. In this case, the formula becomes:

$$\text{Percentage of transfer} = \frac{C - E}{C} \times 100 \qquad (1b)$$

This formula is appropriate with such measures as errors, trials to reach some criterion, or time. It is obvious that as errors, trials, or time are reduced in value, performance improves.

A second type of transfer formula has been proposed by Gagné *et al.* (1948). This procedure compares the difference between the E and C groups with the maximum amount of improvement possible on the transfer task. The maximum improvement possible is indicated by the difference between the total possible score on Task B and the performance of the C group on Task B. If the measure of learning is one such as number of correct responses, as in Formula (1a), and T stands for the total possible score, the formula is:

$$\text{Percentage of transfer} = \frac{E - C}{T - C} \times 100 \qquad (2a)$$

The denominator and numerator are reversed if the measure of learning is one such as time, trials or errors, as in Formula (1b).

$$\text{Percentage of transfer} = \frac{C - E}{C - T} \times 100 \qquad (2b)$$

A chief difficulty with using either Formula (2a) or Formula (2b) is that we do not always know the total possible score T, and its determination may be difficult or impossible.

Murdock (1957) has suggested a third type of transfer formula which has a distinct advantage over the first two described. The maximum amount of positive transfer which can be obtained is 100 per cent transfer and the maximum amount of negative transfer is -100 per cent; in other words, the upper and lower limits are equal, and positive and negative transfer are symmetrical. This is accomplished by making the denominator of the formula include the performance of the E group as well as the C group. The formula is:

$$\text{Percentage of transfer} = \frac{E - C}{E + C} \times 100 \qquad (3a)$$

Like Formula (1a), Formula (3a) is appropriate if the measure of performance is such that the larger the value of the measure, the better the performance. If the measure of performance is such that the smaller the value of the measure, the better the performance, the formula must be modified to read:

$$\text{Percentage of transfer} = \frac{C - E}{E + C} \times 100 \qquad (3b)$$

Comparison of Formulas

A comparison of Formulas (1a), (2a), and (3a) is shown in Table 2. Hypothetical values for E, C, and T are listed along with the percentage transfer obtained with each formula. Because different percentages of transfer are obtained with each formula, the importance of knowing what transfer formula was used in a particular study becomes obvious, especially if one wishes to compare the magnitude and direction of transfer obtained in different studies. This latter point has been strongly emphasized by both Gagné *et al.* (1948) and Murdock (1957).

TABLE 2

Comparison of Percentage Transfer Obtained
by Three Transfer Formulas

Number of Correct Responses			Percentage Transfer from Formula		
E	C	T	(1a)	(2a)	(3a)
50	0	50	+Infinity	+100	+100
25	15	50	+67	+29	+25
15	15	50	0	0	0
15	25	50	−40	−40	−25
0	50	50	−100	−Infinity	−100

CHAPTER III

Transfer and Task Similarity

ASSUME THAT THE RULES GOVERNING TRAFFIC LIGHTS IN our society were suddenly changed so that we no longer stopped our car when the signal light was red but when the light was orange. What would be likely to happen? Would this change in lights be likely to cause difficulty in driving? Probably not. What we have done in this instance is to require our driver to make the *same* response of stopping to stimulus events that are *highly similar*. In other words, since red and orange are similar, it would be relatively easy to learn to stop at an orange light. More generally, learning to make the same response to new but similar stimuli leads to positive transfer.

Now, let us consider a more radical departure from current traffic light regulations. Suppose that instead of stopping the car when the light was red, we had to learn to go when the light was red and to stop with the green light. In other words, we reverse our signals. What is now likely to happen is fairly obvious. Confusion and accidents are reasonably predictable. We now require drivers to make an entirely *new* (in this case, opposite) response to the same stimuli, which is a frequent condition for interference among responses, or negative transfer.

These two hypothetical examples serve to highlight the significance of similarity in transfer of learning. Furthermore, they illustrate something of the importance of understanding the similarity relationships among tasks so as to be able to predict the course of transfer of learning. As indicated in Chapter I, we do not learn in a vacuum—our present learning is influenced by our previous learning.

THE MEANING OF SIMILARITY

A number of studies have shown that similarity between original and transfer tasks is a major factor in influencing the degree of transfer of learning. In general, the greater the degree of similarity between the two tasks, the greater the amount of positive transfer obtained. Although results that conform to this generalization have been obtained in a number of instances, *it is by no means an uncomplicated or simple one.*

First, the generalization is dependent upon the meaning of similarity—that is, the way in which similarity is measured. Similarity is a complex variable in that there are several ways in which it can be defined. In the case of ordinary learning tasks, such as languages, it is fairly obvious that there are several possible dimensions of similarity that may exist. If asked, "How are French and Spanish similar?" it is clear that they are similar in several ways such as in the spelling of certain words, common root language, and in the sound of some of the words. Second, because many learning tasks may be analyzed into both stimulus and response components, tasks may vary along dimensions of either stimulus or response similarity.

In general, similarity has been defined in three ways: (1) scales of similarity have been constructed based upon the judgments of subjects, (2) similarity has been defined in terms of variation along some known physical dimension such as size or intensity, and (3) similarity has been defined in terms of transfer itself, which is most unsatisfactory.

One way of defining the meaningful similarity of verbal materials has been described by Haagen (1949). He presented subjects with a group of paired adjectives, such as "fancy-deluxe," and asked them to judge each pair along a seven-point scale of similarity ranging from very great to very slight similarity. For each pair of adjectives, he obtained an average rating based on the subject's judgments and called this the scale-value for the pair. The scale-values represent the degree of synonymity of verbal pairs that can, in turn, be experimentally manipulated in subsequent studies by selecting appropriate pairs from the list. A sample set of items from Haagen's list is shown below. A standard word is given along with three comparison words which were judged to be relatively high, moderate, and low in similarity to the standard word. For example, "beloved" and "cherished" were judged to be highly similar whereas "beloved" and "preferred" were judged to be relatively low in similarity.

Standard Word	High Similarity	Moderate Similarity	Low Similarity
Beloved	Cherished	Prized	Preferred
Sickly	Unwell	Infirm	Bedfast
Complete	Entire	Utter	Perfect
Urgent	Pressing	Acute	Crying

Verbal materials may also vary along at least two additional dimensions of similarity, homonymity, and antonymity, as well as synonymity (Cofer and Foley, 1942). Homonyms are words with the same sounds but different meanings and antonyms are words with opposite meanings. The fact that meaningful verbal materials can vary along three possible dimensions of similarity increases the difficulty of straight forward manipulation of this variable.

Another way of manipulating the similarity of verbal materials is to vary the letter-elements of nonsense syllables. For example, a nonsense syllable such as CEK might be changed to CIK, a one-letter variation, or CEK might be changed to COZ, a two-letter variation. In other words, we can vary the formal similarity of nonsense syllables in terms of the number of letter-elements which are altered. The more the alteration, the less the similarity between pairs of syllables.

A way of defining the similarity of perceptual materials has been described by Gibson (1941), who constructed a series of figural designs which varied in degree of similarity. These designs consisted of arbitrary figures which were relatively meaningless. Initially, Gibson drew twelve figures to be used as standard stimuli. A large pool of additional figures which were variations of the standard were then drawn. Judges selected from this pool those figures that were similar to each of the standard stimuli and ranked them according to their degree of similarity to the standard. The final set of figures consisted of the twelve standard figures with three other figures of varying degree of similarity to each standard, measured in terms of a procedure Gibson called "generalization." An illustration of a standard figure and its three variations is shown in Figure 1.

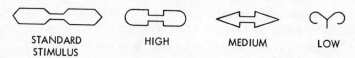

STANDARD   HIGH   MEDIUM   LOW
STIMULUS

FIGURE 1. An illustration of the Gibson figures showing a standard and its variations through three degrees of similarity. (Adapted from Gibson, 1941.)

In order to obtain a measure of "generalization," subjects were given five trials to learn to associate a different nonsense name to each of the standard figures. On the following day, subjects were shown the standard figures, as well as variations of the standard, with instructions to recall their names as quickly as possible. In this fashion, similarity or "generalization" was defined in terms of the frequency with which subjects responded to the variations as if they were the original standard figures. It should be noted that this procedure is not entirely satisfactory because it defines similarity in terms of one possible measure of transfer itself. In order to demonstrate any relation between similarity and transfer it is necessary to have some measure of similarity that is *independent* of the measure of transfer.

Other ways of defining similarity have been in terms of jnd scales of pitch (Hovland, 1937), varying the size of circular stimuli (Grice and Saltz, 1950), number of elements in a task that are changed (Crafts, 1935), error matrices (Rothkopf, 1957), and judged similarity of visual patterns (Yum, 1931, McKinney, 1933), to mention a few. Similarity has been defined in a variety of ways, and attempts to relate similarity and transfer in some lawful and systematic way depend to some extent on the particular way in which similarity is measured.

TRANSFER AND SIMILARITY: AN ILLUSTRATION

The effect of similarity on transfer can easily be illustrated in a study by Ellis (1958). Only a portion of the results will be described. In this study he investigated transfer in verbal learning using the paired-associate technique, which consists of presenting subjects with pairs of words, the first member of the pair being the stimulus and the second member being the response. The subject's task is to learn to associate each response with its stimulus word, so that when he sees the stimulus word alone he can produce the correct response. There is no necessary logical connection between the stimulus and response words and the subject has to discover various cues for associating or "hooking up" the stimulus-response pairs. An example of a stimulus-response pair is "urgent-barren"; the subject would have to learn to say "barren" when presented the word "urgent" by itself.

In the Ellis study, subjects learned an original list of eight paired-associates. After a two-day interval, subjects then learned a second list of paired-associates in which the stimulus words were varied through several degrees of similarity and the responses were kept the same. Examples of pairs of words learned in the original and two of the transfer lists are shown below:

Group	Original List		Transfer List	
I	*Stimuli*	*Responses*	*Stimuli*	*Responses*
(High Stimulus Similarity)	Agile	Modest	Nimble	Modest
	Empty	Unclear	Vacant	Unclear
	Liquid	Weary	Fluid	Weary
II	*Stimuli*	*Responses*	*Stimuli*	*Responses*
(Moderate Stimulus Similarity)	Agile	Modest	Lively	Modest
	Empty	Unclear	Hollow	Unclear
	Liquid	Weary	Flowing	Weary

Subjects learned the original list and only one of the transfer lists of either high or moderate similarity. The words were selected from Haagen's (1949) scale of meaningful similarity, described earlier. For example, agile and nimble were judged to be more similar than agile and lively and, similarly, empty and vacant were judged to be more similar than empty and hollow. On this basis it would be predicted that Group I would learn its transfer list faster than Group II.

Group I, which learned the transfer list of high similarity, averaged 3.2 correct responses on the first test trial of the transfer task, whereas Group II, which learned the moderate similarity list made only 1.4 correct responses on the same trial. Both groups were superior to control groups which made only 0.6 correct responses on the same trial. The results illustrate the principle that the greater the degree of stimulus similarity, the greater the amount of positive transfer.

STIMULUS SIMILARITY AND TRANSFER

A simple type of transfer study is one in which the responses in the original and transfer task are the same but the stimuli are varied. An example of this type of study was seen in the Ellis (1958) experiment. Using Design 1, this type of study in its simplest form can be diagramed as shown below:

	Original Task	*Transfer Task*
Experimental Group	Learn $S_0 - R_0$	Learn $S_1 - R_0$
Control Group	(Rest)	Learn $S_1 - R_0$

In this illustration, the experimental group learns an original task, $S_0 - R_0$, say a paired-associates task, and then learns a transfer task, $S_1 - R_0$. The stimuli in the transfer task S_1 are different from those in the original task—that is, they vary along some dimension of similarity. The responses remain the same in the two tasks, which are symbolized as R_0 in both the original and transfer task.

This type of approach was used in the classic study of Yum (1931). Subjects learned a list of fourteen such paired-associates; as an example of a specific pair, they were taught to say the word "jury" to the stimulus "toq-bex." Twenty-four hours after learning, a test was given in which the stimulus items were varied through several degrees of similarity; for instance, "toq-bex" was changed to "tiq-bex," a change of one letter. A measure was taken of the extent to which the subjects responded to the modified stimuli as if they were the original stimuli. In this instance, *recall*, and not new learning, was measured. Transfer, as measured by the recall of the original response, was always positive, but varied with the degree of similarity in the stimuli. The greater the amount of change in the stimuli —that is, the less their similarity—the less the amount of recall.

Yum repeated this experiment using perceptual as well as verbal materials. In this instance, subjects learned responses to visual patterns and then were tested in an analogous fashion with visual patterns varying through several degrees of similarity. Again, he found that the greater the similarity of the test visual patterns to the original, the greater the likelihood of recall. Table 1 shows the basic results of Yum's two studies.

TABLE 1

Transfer as a Function of Degree of Similarity
Between Stimulus Members [*]

	Percentage Recalled	
Degree of Stimulus Similarity	*Words*	*Visual Patterns*
Word or pattern same	50.15 per cent	84.62 per cent
First-degree similarity	32.56	64.53
Second-degree similarity	11.27	49.15
Third-degree similarity	—	45.30
Fourth-degree similarity	—	36.32

[*] Adapted from Yum (1931).

In very similar studies, both Bruce (1933) and McKinney (1933) obtained results that again confirmed the importance of stimulus similarity in transfer. McKinney required his subjects to learn to associate a particular letter to a particular geometric pattern. After original training, subjects were shown variations of the geometric patterns and were tested for transfer of the same response to these variations. In other words, the question was raised: "To what extent will the subjects give the same response to the altered stimuli, and will the frequency with which they give the same response depend upon the degree of similarity between the variations and the original stimuli?" The results showed quite clearly that the greater the amount of variation with the stimuli, the less frequent the transfer of response.

So far, we have seen that the similarity of verbal materials, and in one instance visual patterns, facilitates positive transfer. Do the results of other studies using visual patterns agree with those using verbal materials? Two significant studies (Gibson, 1941, Hamilton, 1943) demonstrate the role of similarity with visual patterns as stimuli. Hamilton's study required the subjects to associate a non-sense syllable with each of twelve standard patterns (see Figure 1 for examples of the figures). The transfer task required the subjects to associate the same response to variations of the standard stimuli. Stimuli were varied through three degrees of similarity. In Gibson's study, the stimulus items were the same as in Hamilton's study but the transfer list had new responses. In short, the transfer task required subjects to associate different responses to variations of the standard stimuli. In both instances, it can be seen that Design 4 was used. The conditions of the two studies are summarized below:

	Hamilton's Study		Gibson's Study	
Group	Original List	Transfer List	Original List	Transfer List
I	$S_0 - R_0$	$S_0 - R_0$	$S_0 - R_0$	$S_0 - R_x$
II	$S_0 - R_0$	$S_1 - R_0$	$S_0 - R_0$	$S_1 - R_x$
III	$S_0 - R_0$	$S_2 - R_0$	$S_0 - R_0$	$S_2 - R_x$
IV	$S_0 - R_0$	$S_3 - R_0$	$S_0 - R_0$	$S_3 - R_x$

S_1, S_2, and S_3 represent stimuli of decreasing similarity; R_0 in the transfer list indicates the same response is being learned as in the original list and R_x indicates that an entirely new response is being learned. Subjects learned the original and transfer task until they reached a partial criterion of eight out of twelve correct responses. The results of these two studies are summarized in Table 2.

TABLE 2

Transfer of Training as a Function of Degree of Similarity of Visual Patterns [1]

	Mean Trials to Learn 8/12 Responses			
	Hamilton		Gibson	
Group	Original List	Transfer List	Original List	Transfer List
I	6.73	1.27	6.86	7.43
II	7.40	2.08	7.00	5.43
III	7.40	2.35	7.07	5.71
IV	7.44	3.48	7.14	3.93

[1] Adapted from Hamilton (1943) and Gibson (1941).

Comparisons of performance on the original list show that the groups were performing at about the same level. In other words, the groups were comparable prior to the test of transfer, which is to be expected since they were all learning the same task.

Let us examine Hamilton's results first which show the effect of stimulus similarity on transfer when the responses in the two lists are the same. Group I learned the transfer task in slightly more than one trial which is not surprising since this group continued to learn the original list. Group II required 2.08 trials to learn the transfer list, and as the stimuli became less similar with those of the original list, the number of trials to reach criterion increased. It is clear that with increasing similarity there is increasing positive transfer, but this is true *only* when the responses in the two lists remain the *same*. Now, what happens if the responses are new or *different?* Gibson's results answer this question.

Gibson's results indicate that positive transfer decreases with increasing stimulus similarity provided that the responses are different. Group I learns to make new responses to the same stimuli; in this case, learning is most difficult, requiring an average of 7.43 trials to reach criterion. In other words, Group I showed some slight negative transfer—that is, interference in learning its transfer list. Groups II and III, which are of intermediate similarity, require about 5 trials, and Group IV, which has the least similarity, requires the fewest trials to learn the list.

The significance of the Gibson study is that it demonstrates a restriction on the general rule that similarity helps transfer. *If the responses in the transfer task are different from those in the original task, then the greater the similarity of stimuli, the less the transfer.*

A practical, although hypothetical, example will help to make this principle somewhat more obvious. Suppose that the rules governing traffic lights in our society were now changed so that we no longer stopped our car in the presence of a red light and had to learn to go in the presence of an orange light. The situation can be diagramed as shown below:

Old Traffic Rule	*New Traffic Rule*
$S_0 - R_0$	$S_1 - R_x$
Red light $-$ Stop	Orange light $-$ Go

This situation amounts to making a new (in this case opposite) response R_x to a very similar stimulus S_1. Now, what is likely to happen? We would, in all likelihood, find it a bit difficult to learn to go when we saw an orange light. We would be likely to continue to stop because of an earlier learned response of stopping in the presence of a similar light. Orange and red are similar, and would be likely to cause considerable confusion in our driving habits. On the other hand, it would be easier to learn to go in the presence of lights which are less similar to red than is orange.

So far, the experiments have been restricted to paired-associates learning. What generalizations can be drawn with respect to other types of tasks, such as judgmental and perceptual-motor tasks? A study by Heath (1959) sheds some light on the role of similarity on expectancy. In this study, one group of subjects took a test, were given their scores, and were then asked what score they expected to make on a second test on the same subject matter. Six different tests were constructed and then judged according to their similarity to the initial test. The results indicated that the subjects were more likely to obtain a score which was close to their expected score as similarity of the second test to the first test increased.

Duncan (1953) conducted a study in which subjects had to learn to move a stick into a particular slot which was paired with a light of a given hue. After original learning, the position of the light was changed and the subjects had to learn to re-pair the movement of the stick with the new position of the light. The fewer the number of variations in the light-slot pairings the easier it was to learn the new task.

TRANSFER AND STIMULUS GENERALIZATION

At this point the reader may observe that transfer based on stimulus similarity appears related to the phenomena of stimulus generalization. Indeed, the simplest form of transfer is stimulus generalization. Empirically, transfer and stimulus generalization are instances of the same class of events. On more formal grounds, stimulus generalization has been used as the theoretical basis for explaining transfer; however, Guttman (1963) has recently objected to this use of generalization by contending that both transfer and generalization are related phenomena that themselves need explanation in terms of more fundamental concepts. Our chief interest is to note their empirical similarity, regardless of divergencies in theoretical views.

Stimulus generalization is defined by the fact that when a response is conditioned to a particular stimulus, stimuli which possess related characteristics also acquire some capacity to elicit the response. Stimulus generalization has been reliably demonstrated in a number of studies (for example, Hovland, 1937, Guttman and Kalish, 1956), and our only purpose is to briefly compare generalization and transfer. Stimulus generalization is usually measured in a few test trials and is the evocation of a nonreinforced response given to stimuli similar to the conditioned stimulus. In contrast, transfer concerns the acquisition of new responses or the attachment of old responses to new stimuli. Stimulus generalization is most similar to performance on the first trial in a test of transfer. In short, transfer and generalization may be measured in different ways and probably reflect different aspects of some more common process.

RESPONSE SIMILARITY AND TRANSFER

Suppose that you are a beginning student of German and you read a passage that contains the word *schule*. In all likelihood, you will be able to guess correctly at its meaning, which is school. This is an instance of positive transfer based on the similarity of the two response words. More generally, transfer between English and related languages, such as German, is based upon the possession of cognates, words which look or sound very much alike. Unfortunately, extensive reliance upon cognates to aid in translation may lead to errors. For example, the German word *wand* does not mean the same as its English counterpart; rather, wand means wall. Thus, although the concept of response similarity may seem reasonably clear, the scaling of response similarity, with few exceptions, has proved to be an even more complicated task than that of scaling stimulus similarity.

What happens when we require a person to make new responses to the same stimuli? There is an old rule of thumb (Bruce, 1933, Wylie, 1919) that says that this situation will lead to interference or negative transfer. Presumably, the responses learned in the first task will interfere or compete with the new responses to be learned in the transfer task. Unfortunately, the results on this issue are somewhat complicated, and we shall see that *both* positive and negative transfer can result in this situation. The fact that both types of transfer can occur suggests that additional factors in the learning situation

besides those of similarity may determine the direction and magnitude of transfer.

The study of response similarity as a factor in transfer usually takes the form of having subjects learn an initial task, $S_0 - R_0$, and then learn a transfer task, $S_0 - R_1$. The stimuli in the two tasks are kept identical, whereas the responses are varied, frequently through several degrees of judged similarity. Using Design 1, this type of study in its simplest form is diagramed below:

	Original Task	*Transfer Task*
Experimental Group	Learn $S_0 - R_0$	Learn $S_0 - R_1$
Control Group	(Rest)	Learn $S_0 - R_1$

A study by Underwood [1] [1] used this type of approach. He had subjects learn an initial paired-associate list of adjectives and then learn a second list in which the stimulus items were kept the same but the responses were varied through three degrees of similarity: high, moderate, and low. Response similarity was manipulated by selecting items from Haagen's (1949) list of adjectives. In addition, three variations in the degrees of first-list learning were introduced by having subjects learn to a criterion of either four correct responses out of twelve, seven out of twelve, or perfect mastery of the list. In summary, three conditions of response similarity were used with each of three degrees of learning of the original list, making a total of nine conditions of the experiment.

The basic results of performance on the transfer list are shown in Table 3. This table shows the mean number of trials to reach criterion on the transfer list as a function of response similarity and degree of first-list learning. The table indicates that with increasing similarity of responses, fewer trials are required to learn the transfer list. For example, the group which learned the initial list to a criterion of perfect mastery required only 3.17 trials to reach criterion on the transfer list of high similarity, whereas the low similarity group took 6.33 trials, almost twice as many. In all cases, however, transfer was positive. The table also indicates that the effects of response similarity are not so pronounced with smaller amounts of first-list learning.

[1] Bracketed numbers refer to readings in Part Two.

TABLE 3

Mean Trials to Reach Criterion on the Transfer List as a
Function of Response Similarity and Degree of First-List Learning [*]

Response Similarity	Degree of First-List Learning		
	4/12	7/12	Perfect Mastery
High	5.50	4.56	3.17
Moderate	6.28	6.56	4.72
Low	6.78	6.94	6.33

[*] Adapted from Underwood [1].

Underwood performed an additional analysis of the transfer data by examining performance on the first-anticipation trial of the transfer list. He reasoned, in terms of a theory of response generalization, that the likelihood of making a correct response on the first anticipation trial should vary with the degree of response similarity. His results supported his reasoning in that the percentage of correct responses on the first trial was found to increase with increasing response similarity. For further details of the study the reader should consult Part Two.

Underwood's study indicates evidence for positive transfer when subjects learned to make new responses to the same stimuli, a finding that appears to contradict the old rule of thumb that says that this situation should lead to negative transfer. A study by Porter and Duncan (1953) throws some light on this finding because both positive and negative transfer were obtained, depending upon the conditions of the experiment.

First, when subjects were simply required to make new responses to the same stimuli in a paired-associate task, positive transfer was obtained just as in Underwood's study. In this instance, part of the positive transfer can be explained as a result of general practice effects of simply learning how to learn this material. If the second list, however, consists not of new responses to be made to the same stimuli, but rather of the same responses as in the original list repaired with the same stimuli, negative transfer results. In this instance, the same responses were being learned in the second list but paired with different stimuli. Interference was great because the original stimulus-response associations competed with those of the second list. It should be noted that negative transfer is usually difficult to obtain in verbal learning, except under conditions in which the same responses are re-paired in the transfer list. On the other hand, negative transfer is frequently seen in motor skills learning where new responses must be attached to old stimuli.

So far, the experiments discussed have described the effect of either stimulus or response similarity on transfer with the exception of Gibson's (1941) study which varied both simultaneously. What happens when both stimuli and responses are varied? It will be recalled that Gibson found that if the responses in the transfer task are quite different from those in the original task, then the greater the degree of stimulus similarity, the *less* the amount of positive transfer. In other words, the Gibson study showed that stimulus similarity hindered rather than helped transfer when responses were varied.

Osgood's Transfer Surface

In 1949 Osgood [2] presented a model of transfer based on the effects of stimulus and response similarity. His review of the transfer literature led him to make three empirical generalizations, sometimes referred to as Osgood's laws of transfer, regarding the effects of similarity on both transfer and interference effects in retention. Only the transfer effects will be considered. Sometimes Osgood's laws are referred to as a theory of transfer; they are best understood, however, as *empirical generalizations* based upon known experimental evidence. In other words, Osgood's laws and the model based upon them are descriptive statements that summarize the known facts about transfer. They do not represent theory in the more formal sense.

The three types of transfer studies, usually referred to as *transfer paradigms,* that have been described so far are summarized in Table 4. Paradigm *A* describes the situation in which the stimuli in the transfer task are varied and the responses are the same as those in the original task. The studies which vary only stimulus similarity fit this paradigm (for example, Yum, 1931, McKinney, 1933, Hamilton, 1943). Paradigm *B* describes the situation in which the responses in the transfer task are varied but the stimuli are kept the same. The studies which vary only response similarity fit this paradigm (for example, Underwood [1], Porter and Duncan, 1953). Finally, Paradigm *C* describes the situation in which both stimuli and responses are varied in some degree of similarity (for example, Gibson, 1941).

TABLE 4

Transfer of Training Paradigms [*]

Paradigm	Original Task	Transfer Task
A	$S_0 - R_0$	$S_1 - R_0$
B	$S_0 - R_0$	$S_0 - R_1$
C	$S_0 - R_0$	$S_1 - R_1$

[*] Adapted from Osgood [2].

Based upon the existing empirical evidence on these transfer paradigms, Osgood made three generalizations about transfer that are summarized below. (1) In the case of Paradigm A, where the stimuli are varied and the responses are kept the same, we find that positive transfer increases with increasing stimulus similarity. (2) With Paradigm B, where the responses are varied and the stimuli are the same, we find that negative transfer is obtained which decreases as the similarity between the responses increases. (3) With Paradigm C, where both stimuli and responses are varied, negative transfer is obtained, which increases as the similarity of the stimuli increases.

All three of these generalizations can be represented in a three-dimensional form as shown in Figure 5 of Osgood [2]. This figure represents the effect of stimulus and response similarity on degree of transfer. The vertical dimension represents degree of transfer going from maximum positive through zero to maximum negative transfer. Stimulus similarity is shown along a second dimension and response similarity is shown along a third dimension. The rectangular plane, which is anchored on the left at the point of zero transfer, represents zero transfer throughout the surface. The curved portion of the surface is used to indicate whether positive or negative transfer is to be obtained. The amount of transfer in a given situation is determined by knowing both the degree of stimulus and response similarity. We project the degree of stimulus similarity and the degree of response similarity until the projections intersect and then determine whether the point of intersection is above or below the zero reference plane. If it is above the reference plane, transfer is positive; if it is below, transfer is negative; if it coincides with the plane, transfer is zero.

For example, we see from this figure that the conditions for maximum positive transfer consist of a transfer task having stimuli and responses which are identical to those of the original task. This is reasonable because it indicates that the transfer task is merely a continuation of the original learning task. Also, as long as the responses are identical, almost any degree of stimulus similarity will yield some positive transfer. The condition for maximum negative transfer is having to make antagonistic responses to identical stimuli. Also, the figure indicates that if *highly* similar responses are made to the same stimuli, positive transfer will occur. In other words, making new responses to the same stimuli does not always lead to negative transfer.

SOME LIMITATIONS OF THE OSGOOD SURFACE

Some limitations of the Osgood surface should be noted. First, the model is restricted to those transfer studies which vary stimulus or response similarity. It is not applicable to learning situations in which the tasks cannot be analyzed into separate stimulus and response components. It does not take into account additional variables such as amount of learning or related phenomena such as learning to learn. Its adequacy is dependent upon our measures of similarity which are not too well developed (Greenspoon, 1963).

On logical grounds, the Osgood surface faces additional difficulty. We see from the figure that, in general, making a different response to the same stimuli predicts negative transfer, except when the responses are highly similar. When the responses are highly similar, positive transfer is predicted, a finding obtained by Underwood [1]. But how are we to know *a priori* where we are on the dimension of response similarity? How are we to know if responses are similar, highly similar or, perhaps, almost identical? Unless we can measure similarity in some adequate fashion, it is difficult to use the model for predictive purposes.

In addition, Osgood's surface is not entirely supported by the existing data. Bugelski and Cadwallader (1956) conducted a rather elaborate experiment to test Osgood's transfer surface. Subjects learned paired-associate lists using the Gibson figures as stimuli and words as responses and then learned transfer lists which were varied with respect to both stimulus and response similarity. The results with respect to stimulus similarity were generally in accord with Osgood's surface. In contrast, the findings with respect to response similarity were not in accord with Osgood's predictions. When the subjects learned to make different responses, varying along a dimension of response similarity, to the same stimuli, there was no systematic decrease in transfer as the responses became less similar. As Underwood (1961) has noted, however, Bugelski and Cadwallader's findings might be the result of differences in difficulty among the transfer lists. The design was such that all subjects learned a common original list and different transfer lists (Design 4, as described in Chapter II), and no determination was made of the difficulty of the various transfer lists themselves.

In a recent study, Dallet (1962) partially replicated the study of Bugelski and Cadwallader and obtained results that were in somewhat better agreement with the predictions of the Osgood surface. For the moment, at least, the portion of the surface that deals with response similarity needs further examination. Finally, the development of more adequate conceptual models of transfer will occur only after we have developed better ways of measuring stimulus and response similarity.

CHAPTER IV

The Transfer of General Factors

SO FAR WE HAVE CONSIDERED STUDIES THAT INVOLVE some type of dimensional variation of similarity and its effect upon transfer. There are several additional kinds of transfer phenomena that are also a function of the similarity between tasks. In these tasks, however, the dimensions of similarity have not been analyzed in any explicit fashion or in the manner in which similarity has been described in the previous section. These related transfer phenomena include learning to learn, warm-up, mediation, non-specific transfer, and bilateral transfer. In all instances, the transfer observed in these phenomena is a function of gross similarity relationships even though the specific dimensions of similarity either have not or cannot be analyzed in any simple fashion. An analysis of learning to learn will quickly illustrate this point.

LEARNING TO LEARN

It is commonly observed that individuals improve in their ability to learn new tasks when they have practiced a series of related or similar tasks. For example, if a person practices solving linear equations each day for several days, he becomes progressively more efficient in solving linear equations. He not only becomes more accurate in his work, but he solves the problems much faster. This progressive improvement in performance is a form of transfer known as *learning to learn*. The phenomena of learning to learn can be observed in a variety of tasks ranging from rote learning to problem solving. The similarity relationships involved appear to be learning general approaches or modes of attack, becoming familiar with the situation, and learning related classes of materials.

A study by Ward (1937) illustrates learning to learn. He required subjects to learn successive lists of nonsense syllables, one list a day. Each list contained twelve syllables, and they were approximately equal in difficulty. Ward's results indicate that subjects required approximately thirty-eight trials to completely master the first list. After six lists, subjects required only twenty trials to reach mastery, and after fifteen lists, subjects required about fourteen trials to master the list. Improvement was most rapid during the first six lists and was more gradual afterwards. It is clear, of course, that subjects learned how to learn this type of material even though it consisted of relatively meaningless nonsense syllables.

Similar results were obtained in a study by Melton and Von Lackum (1941). Subjects learned words and numbers as well as nonsense syllables and continued to show improvement in learning to learn over relatively long practice periods. Marx (1944) has demonstrated cumulative transfer of learning to learn in rats. Rats were put through a series of similar water mazes and were observed to continue to improve in running subsequent mazes. Like Ward's findings, the greatest amount of improvement occurred early in the series and although improvement continued, the gains became progressively smaller. Similar results were obtained by Bunch (1944) in maze learning with college students.

Although learning to learn was a well-established principle, the series of experiments by Harlow [3] [1] served to call attention to the widespread importance of this principle and to its relevance to much of human learning. In the typical Harlow experiment, monkeys are trained on relatively simple discrimination problems. For example, a monkey is presented with two objects, a cube and a solid triangle, with a raisin always being under one and never the other. The position of the cube and triangle is randomized so that the monkey must learn which of two stimuli hides the raisin. After the monkey masters this discrimination problem he is presented another. This time he might have to learn to discriminate between a small cube and a large cube, again with the raisin always being

[1] Bracketed numbers refer to readings in Part Two.

under one stimulus. Successive discrimination problems are given and it is observed that the monkeys become progressively more efficient—for example, faster, in learning the discrimination problem. After hundreds of practice trials on successive discrimination problems, monkeys learn to solve new discrimination problems extremely fast. Harlow contends that the animal has learned how to learn this problem—that is, he has acquired a learning set for this class of problems. Subsequently, Harlow demonstrated the same kind of results with young children.

Harlow's findings have significant implications for education. Learning-set theory implies that important aspects of learning how to learn to solve problems are built up over many practice trials on related problems. It is only after extensive practice that the child becomes proficient in executing complex skills and in solving problems. Casual or haphazard instruction in basic skills is obviously not the way in which important concepts or skills are reliably acquired. This point has also been recognized by Skinner (1954 and 1958), who argues that programed instruction represents an extremely efficient way for the learning of many concepts and principles. It is sufficient at this point to note that a relevant feature of programed instruction is that it gives the student extensive practice on a series of related problems and carefully leads the student toward the development of concepts.

In the development of learning sets, Harlow has sometimes arranged the experimental situation so that the cues are reversed. If the positive cue was originally the cube instead of the triangle, the triangle is now made the positive cue—that is, the stimulus under which the raisin is placed. It will be recalled that, according to Osgood's transfer surface, this is a condition for producing negative transfer. At first, this is precisely what happens. The animal has some difficulty in dealing with the reversed cues and continues to select the original cue. Later, after considerable practice in dealing with reversals, he acquires a facility for handling them and learns to shift with relative ease. In short, the animal becomes flexible in dealing with discrimination reversals. One educational implication stemming from this finding is that if we wish to teach children to be flexible in problem solving, then they must be given practice with various tasks in which cue reversal occurs.

Later, Harlow (1959) noted that the early trials are extremely significant in establishing a reliable learning-set. He contends that if practice with a particular type of problem is discontinued before it is reliably learned, then little transfer will occur to the next series of problems. Therefore, he concludes that considerable time and effort should be spent on the early problems before moving on to more complex problems. As a learning-set becomes more securely developed, relatively few trials are necessary on new problems.

Harlow's findings also suggest a possible explanation for the behavioral phenomenon of "insight." Generally, insight refers to the rapid solution of a problem. In view of Harlow's findings, it would appear that insight might be a result of extensive practice on related problems. In other words, insight is a phenomenon which is seen as a result of learning to learn.

Finally, Harlow suggests that the concept of learning-set is applicable to the development of social-emotional behavior as well as problem solving. The development of personality characteristics, he feels, is the result of the formation of particular learning sets. For further details, the reader should examine Harlow's paper in Part Two.

WARM-UP

A phenomenon related to learning to learn is *warm-up*. A basic difference between the two, however, is that warm-up is a much more transitory or short-lived effect. The effect of warm-up on subsequent learning can be seen in a study by Hamilton (1950). He required subjects to learn a paired-associate list of meaningful words and then gave them another list, a test list, with varying intervals of time elapsing between the initial and test list. The results of learning the test list showed that it was easier to learn if practiced soon after the initial list, within about sixty minutes, but that the facilitating effects were smaller and rather constant after a sixty-minute interval between lists. This transitory facilitation in learning transfer tasks is evidence for the warm-up effect. Similar results have been shown by Thune (1950), who was able to isolate warm-up and learning-to-learn effects in a single experiment.

NONSPECIFIC TRANSFER

Nonspecific transfer is a general concept that refers to transfer not dependent upon any specific features of the task, but dependent upon more general characteristics, such as of modes of attack and general principles. Learning to learn and warm-up are instances of nonspecific transfer. In the case of paired-associate learning, the A–B, C–D paradigm is also an instance of nonspecific transfer. In this case, the transfer list consists of entirely new stimulus-response pairs that are unrelated to the pairs in the original list. Thus, any positive transfer or facilitation in learning the transfer list is due, not to specific features of the list, but to more general features such as learning-how-to-learn paired-associate lists.

MEDIATIONAL PROCESSES IN TRANSFER

The extent to which persons learn a new task depends to some degree upon individual learner characteristics. When faced with a new task, the ease with which it is learned will depend upon past experiences of the learner and how these experiences are utilized in the present task. If, for example, we ask a person to "think of an example of negative transfer," we may observe that he delays his answer for a few seconds and then may give us a reply. During this delay, certain intervening processes are taking place, which we usually refer to as thinking. In essence, however, the learner is making certain nonverbalized responses to the question which in turn ultimately leads to an answer. We call these intervening processes *mediating responses* because they serve to bridge the gap or mediate between the question presented and the final answer produced. Sometimes learners are quite aware of mediating processes —that is, they can verbalize about them, and in other instances learners appear to be unaware of any mediational processes taking place.

From our point of view, mediating responses are to be regarded as mechanisms for producing transfer. In other words, the ease or difficulty with which a person learns a new task depends in part upon the kind of mediating responses which are available, these in turn being a function of earlier learning experiences. Much of the ability of humans to learn new tasks with ease stems from their use of language, a major source of mediating responses. In fact, a chief difference between humans and lower animals is in their ability to use language to help mediate new behavior.

An experiment by Bugelski and Scharlock (1952) demonstrated how language serves as a mediating response in learning a paired-associate list of words. They showed that the ease of learning a paired-associate list was dependent upon having learned previous lists which contained responses which would facilitate or *mediate* the learning of a third list. For example, learning an initial pair of words such as "fish-hat," and then learning a second pair such as "hat-book," in which the response word in the first list became the stimulus word in the second list, facilitated the learning of a third pair, "fish-book."

Russell and Storms [4], in a classic paper, have demonstrated the role of *associative frequency* in mediating the learning of a new task. In this study, several mediating responses related to each other—that is, chains of responses—were used to demonstrate transfer effects. Words were selected from the Kent-Rosanoff list, which is made up of words that are commonly associated. Briefly, the Kent-Rosanoff list was constructed by presenting subjects with a large number of words and having them respond as fast as they could with an association. By selecting words from the Kent-Rosanoff list, Russell and Storms could infer the likelihood of a given association to a stimulus word, and by knowing that a given response had a given associative probability, a chain of associates was selected. For example, by looking at the word "stem" in the Kent-Rosanoff list, they knew that the most frequent associative response was "flower." In turn, the most frequent associative response to "flower" was "smell." They reasoned that if subjects learned a paired-associate list in which they learned to make the response "stem" to the stimulus item "cef"—that is, "cef-stem"—that it would then be easier to learn a new stimulus pair "cef-smell" because of the *chain of associations* known to exist between "stem" and "smell," than it would be to learn another pair "cef-joy" because "joy" had no known associative connection to STEM.

TABLE 1

Schematic Outline of the Conditions of the Experiment *

	Original List	Inferred Chain	Transfer List
Experimental Group	Learn *A–B*	*B–C–D*	Learn *A–D*
Control Group	Learn *A–B*	*B–C–D*	Learn *A–X*

* Adapted from Russell and Storms [4].

A schematic outline of the experiment is shown in Table 1. Subjects in the experimental and control groups learned the same initial list of paired-associates, A–B. The associative chain, B–C–D, is known to already exist, based on data from the Kent-Rosanoff list. It is reasoned that A–D will be easier to learn than A–X, because of the known chain of associations going from B to D. The results confirmed their reasoning. The A–D list was significantly easier to learn, presumably because of the associative connections from B to D. Similarly, Buzzota (1956) in an unpublished study, reported similar findings in a study of mediated transfer. The essential difference between the two studies was that Buzzota experimentally produced the associative linkage rather than infer its existence from a previous word association study.

Finally, it should be noted that studies designed to demonstrate the specific effects of mediation itself, as distinct from other possible sources of transfer, have not always succeeded. For example, Barclay (1963) and Crawford and Vanderplas (1959) all failed to demonstrate any mediation effects in paired-associate learning over and above that which could be attributed to nonspecific transfer. Similarly, Palermo (1962) found in a paired-associate study that the condition designed to produce facilitation in a transfer list through mediated associations was actually inferior to a control group which could not benefit from mediated associations. Although these and similar studies do not invalidate the concept of mediation, they do indicate that the positive transfer effects due to mediation may be masked by other factors or may depend upon the presence or absence of other factors.

BILATERAL TRANSFER

If a person practices a skill such as throwing darts with his right hand, there is usually some positive transfer to his left hand even though no specific practice with the left hand occurs. This transfer from a member on one side of the body to its opposite is called bilateral transfer. Instances of bilateral transfer are fairly common in everyday learning. For example, if you normally write with your right hand, you can also write with your left hand, although with considerably less skill.

V

Additional Factors Influencing Transfer

THIS CHAPTER IS CONCERNED WITH SEVERAL ADDITIONAL factors which influence transfer of learning. In addition to task similarity, transfer depends upon other conditions; however, these factors are to a certain extent secondary in their influence because their effects do depend upon the similarity relationships involved. These factors are: (1) time interval elapsing between tasks, (2) degree of original-task learning, (3) variety of previous tasks, and (4) task difficulty.

TIME INTERVAL BETWEEN TASKS

What happens if the time interval between the original and transfer task is several days or weeks rather than just one day? Does transfer to a subsequent task decline with the passage of time, as does retention, or are the findings more complex? In a series of studies Bunch and his colleagues addressed themselves to this question. A number of their studies (for example, Bunch, 1936, Bunch and McCraven, 1938, Bunch and Lang, 1939) have indicated that transfer of training remains *roughly constant* with varying intervals of time elapsing between the original and transfer tasks. Within the time limits employed, transfer was quite stable and appeared to be remarkably independent of any memory of the original task. This finding is somewhat paradoxical if one takes the view that the amount of transfer from the original to the transfer task is, in a certain sense, one possible measure of retention of the original task. It would certainly appear that if a task is gradually forgotten in the course of time, its transfer to a subsequent task would also decline in the course of time. As indicated, however, the results do not suggest this.

In one of the first of a series of studies on the transfer-time problem Bunch (1936) required subjects to learn a problem-solving task to a criterion of two perfect trials, and then tested independent groups of subjects at 0, 2, 14, 30, or 90 days afterward, requiring them to learn another problem-solving task of the identical type to the same criterion. Additional groups of subjects were tested for their retention of the original task at the same time intervals so that the temporal course of transfer and retention could be compared. A comparison of transfer and retention using *trials* to reach criterion revealed that the percentage transfer remained strikingly similar regardless of the time interval between tasks. Some variation in transfer existed, but it was not systematic or reliable. There was as much transfer after thirty or ninety days as there was immediately after learning the original task. Analogous findings were obtained with the error measures. In contrast, retention measured with either trials or errors showed a decrease with the passage of time between tasks. Although retention declined with the passage of time, the ability of the subjects to transfer their learning to the new task remained roughly the same regardless of the time intervals elapsing between tasks.

In a similar study, Bunch and McCraven (1938) extended this type of problem to the investigation of memory material. Subjects learned an initial list of paired-associate nonsense syllables to complete mastery and then learned a second list to the same criterion after intervals of 0, 2, 14 or 28 days. An *A–B, C–D* transfer paradigm was employed, in which the stimuli and responses in the transfer task were unrelated to those of the original task. An examination of the results revealed that subjects required approximately the same number of trials to master the transfer task, regardless of the time interval separating the tasks. In order to check the reliability of their findings, Bunch and McCraven repeated this study using new subjects and new lists of nonsense syllables. The results were quite comparable to those of the initial experiment. After 0, 2, 14, or 28 days subjects learned transfer lists in 10.95, 10.70, 11.53, and 10.50 trials, respectively, for the different intervals of time. Again, the striking finding of the study was that regardless of the time interval separating the tasks, transfer to the subsequent task remained roughly constant.

In a later study, Gladis (1960) obtained results that were in agreement with those of Bunch. Using school children of various ages, he found that transfer of training remained roughly constant with intervals of 0, 2, and 14 days elapsing between the tasks. The age factor was important in that the older children showed greater amounts of positive transfer.

Bunch (1939) has noted one exception to the stability of the transfer-time function. Under conditions designed to yield negative transfer, in which the cues were reversed in a maze learning task, transfer was found to vary with the passage of time. Negative transfer effects were greatest after short time intervals, but the effect gradually shifted to positive transfer with longer intervals of time.

More recent studies by Ellis and his colleagues have sought to determine the conditions under which transfer remains invariant with time. First, Ellis and Burnstein (1960) demonstrated that the temporal course of transfer declines with an A–B, C–B paradigm— that is, when subjects are required to make the same response to different but similar stimuli in the transfer task. This finding seems reasonable because performance on the transfer task depends partly on the retention of the original responses with this paradigm. Subsequent studies (Ellis and Hunter, 1960, 1961a, and 1961b) demonstrated that under conditions of nonspecific transfer (A–B, C–D paradigm), transfer remains constant with the passage of time. In addition, transfer of training with the A–B, C–B paradigm remains fairly constant if the response items in the task are highly meaningful, or if they are highly familiarized nonsense-syllable responses.

More generally, the findings of Bunch and Ellis, taken together, reveal that transfer of training remains approximately constant as long as performance on the transfer task does not depend on memory for specific items in the original task. Where transfer does depend on memory for specific items, or under conditions of cue reversal, transfer will vary as a function of time elapsing between tasks.

Degree of Original Learning

The results concerning the effects of degree of original learning on transfer are fairly systematic. A general rule of thumb is that positive transfer increases with increasing practice on the original task. Mandler (1962) has summarized the research on this variable and notes that with small amounts of practice there is frequently a negative transfer effect, then a return to zero transfer with more practice, and increasing positive transfer with even more practice. More generally, then, the results reveal a U-shaped function relating degree of original learning and amount of transfer.

The early study of Siipola and Israel (1933) illustrates the effects of varying degrees of original learning on transfer. Subjects learned to pair various telegraph codes to letters of the alphabet as stimuli. The transfer task required learning new code-alphabet combinations. Four degrees of original learning were given: 12, 26, 96, and 208 trials prior to the transfer task. With 12 practice trials, there was slight positive transfer; with 26 trials, negative transfer occurred; and with 96 and 208 trials, increased positive transfer was obtained.

An examination of the Underwood [1] [1] study described in Chapter III reveals much the same effect; however, in this instance, all transfer was positive. Reexamination of Table 3 reveals that with increased amount of practice on the original list, there is an increasing amount of positive transfer that is reflected in the relative ease in which subjects learn the transfer task. Similar findings were obtained by Underwood (1949), although some initial negative transfer resulted from few trials on the original task. With increased practice, there was increased positive transfer. Analogous findings in animal learning were obtained by both Bruner, Mandler, O'Dowd, and Wallach (1958) and by Reid (1953).

Finally, Mandler and Heinemann (1956) conducted a study in which subjects learned nonsense syllables as responses to one-digit numbers. Subjects were given ten, thirty, and fifty trials beyond a criterion of mastery. On the transfer task, subjects showed some initial negative transfer after ten overlearning trials, less negative transfer after thirty overlearning trials and positive transfer after fifty trials.

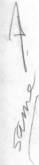

[1] Bracketed numbers refer to readings in Part Two.

Recently, a study by Postman (1962) examined the generalization that positive transfer increases with degree of first-list learning. Postman noted that this generalization, as far as verbal transfer is concerned, holds true as long as the responses are highly similar (Underwood [1]), with a control condition requiring only a single list to be learned (Bruce, 1933) and in studies using the A–B, A–C paradigm, in which the specific and nonspecific transfer are not separated (Atwater, 1953, Underwood, 1949). Postman proposed that the effects of degree of first-list learning be determined using several transfer paradigms, with a nonspecific transfer group being used as a control to evaluate the other transfer paradigms.

Subjects learned one of four different paired-associate lists in which both stimuli and responses were selected from Haagen's (1949) list. The list conformed to four different transfer paradigms: (1) new stimuli and new responses—that is, nonspecific transfer (A–B, C–D); (2) new stimuli and old responses (A–B, C–B); (3) old stimuli and new responses (A–B, A–C); (4) old stimuli and old responses re-paired (A–B, A–Br). Subjects learned a list of ten paired-associates to three different degrees of first-list learning: (1) to a criterion of six out of ten correct responses; (2) perfect mastery; and (3) perfect mastery plus 50 per cent overlearning. Following the various conditions of original learning, subjects learned the same transfer lists. When compared against the nonspecific transfer control (A–B, C–D), all paradigms yielded negative transfer. The amount of negative transfer was greatest for the A–B, A–Br condition, intermediate for the A–B, A–C condition, and least for the A–B, C–B condition. With increased amount of practice on the original task, the A–B, A–Br group continued to yield increasing negative transfer, but with the other groups, negative transfer increased at first and then began to decrease. Although the curves did not show a return to positive transfer, the findings suggest the usual U-shaped function. Perhaps if additional practice had been given transfer would have become positive.

An important educational implication regarding the role of degree of original learning should be noted. All in all, the findings suggest that the greatest amount of negative transfer is likely to occur after relatively little practice on the original task, supporting, in one sense, the old maxim that "a little learning is dangerous." With extensive practice on the original task one runs much less risk of negative transfer. Finally, these generalizations are consistent with those of Harlow, who, as we have seen before, has argued that considerable practice should be given on the early problems of a series in order to maximize transfer in discrimination learning.

VARIETY OF PREVIOUS TASKS

In order to maximize transfer, should one practice extensively on a single task or less on several related tasks? In other words, is practice with a variety of tasks or stimuli an important factor in transfer? This question is of practical as well as of theoretical importance because educational practices such as the optimal design of learning sequences depend upon knowing an answer to this question. It will be recalled that studies of learning to learn (Harlow [3]) indicate that practice on a series of related problems leads to successive improvement in performance; however, these studies do not separate the effects of amount of practice from those of variety of practice. Unfortunately, not a great deal is known about this factor although it is frequently assumed that some degree of variety in the original task will lead to greater positive transfer (Crafts, 1927).

A recent study by Duncan [5] illustrated the separate effects of sheer amount of practice from those of variety of practice on transfer, and showed that task variety is an important factor in producing positive transfer. Subjects were given practice in a perceptual-motor task which required them to learn to place a lever in one of thirteen slots, each slot being separately identified by a number. The subject's task was to learn to place the lever in a particular slot when presented with a particular stimulus item which appeared on a memory drum. The transfer task required the subject to learn to place the lever in the appropriate slot in the presence of *new* stimuli. Two types of stimuli were employed: *H* figures and nonsense syllables. The stimulus-slot pairs were, of course, arbitrary so the task is essentially a paired-associate motor task.

The results can be summarized as follows: (1) the amount of transfer increased as a result of increased amount of practice, and (2) transfer increased as a direct function of increased variety of original training. The improvement in transfer as a result of increased variety of practice was most marked in going from only one to two types of tasks; the increase in transfer was somewhat less in going from two to five to ten different tasks. In other words, the increased positive transfer due to task variety occurred with only a small increase in the number of training tasks.

TRANSFER AND TASK DIFFICULTY

Does preliminary training on an easy or a more difficult task result in greater transfer? Unfortunately, it is somewhat difficult to generalize about the role of task difficulty in transfer. In some instances transfer from an easy to a hard task is greater, and sometimes the reverse occurs. One factor which makes it difficult to generalize about task difficulty is that many different kinds of tasks have been used to vary this dimension (Day, 1956). Because it is not easy to know what constitutes comparable levels of difficulty with different tasks, generalizations about task difficulty tend to be complex.

Lordahl and Archer (1958) examined the effect of practicing at one speed on a pursuit-rotor device and transferring to another speed. The subjects practiced tracking on a pursuit-rotor device at speeds of forty, sixty, or eighty revolutions per minute on the first day and then practiced at sixty revolutions per minute on the second day. The results indicated that subjects who had preliminary practice at either forty or eighty revolutions per minute did significantly poorer on the transfer task than did those who practiced at sixty revolutions per minute. In short, the more similar the original task was to the transfer task, the better the performance on the transfer task. If original training was *either* easier or more difficult, transfer was negative. In a follow-up study, Namikas and Archer (1960) tested the hypothesis that variation of the intertask interval might affect the amount of negative transfer obtained. The training conditions of the earlier study were repeated, but with four time intervals between the two tasks. Again, the findings indicated that transferring to the same speed gave the best performance.

Noble (1959) has raised the question of task difficulty in verbal transfer of training and notes that one way of varying the difficulty of verbal tasks is to manipulate the *meaningfulness* of verbal lists. He gave two groups of subjects lists of verbal materials to learn, one high and one low in meaningfulness, and then tested for transfer with varying types of lists. Subjects learning the high meaning lists learned significantly faster than those who learned the low meaning list. In contrast, on a test of transfer in which subjects learned a new list of items low in meaning, there was no difference in performance as a function of preliminary training. Tentatively, Noble proposed the generalization that meaningfulness facilitates the rate of learning but has no effect on transfer.

A study of Goldstein and Newton (1962) indicated that training on a difficult task led to greater transfer. They used a rather complex tracking task with varying amounts of lag in the control system of the task. What is meant by lag is variation in the time between the subject's movement of a lever and the subsequent response of the system. The task of the subject was to keep a moving pointer on the zero point of a scale by appropriate manipulation of the lever. Variations in the degree of control lag were regarded as variations in task difficulty. The results indicated that performance on the most difficult training task led to the greatest amount of transfer on a subsequent tracking task.

In other tasks, training on an easy task produces greater transfer than does training on a more difficult task. Lawrence (1952) conducted a study of discrimination learning in rats in which animals were trained to discriminate between two brightness levels. One group of animals was given preliminary training with difficult discriminations to make in which the two brightnesses were very similar. Another group started training with easy discriminations in which the two brightnesses were quite different. Following preliminary training all animals were trained on the difficult discrimination which was the transfer test. The results indicated that animals trained on the easy discriminations performed better on the transfer test than those trained originally on the more difficult discrimination. Similarly, in a study of transfer in rotary pursuit tracking, Ammons, Ammons, and Morgan (1956) obtained results which indicated that going from an easy to a difficult task facilitated transfer.

It would appear that systematic generalizations about the role of task difficulty will not be possible until greater attention is given to the concept of difficulty. Also, greater progress in resolving this issue might occur if research stemmed from more theoretically-developed notions of difficulty and if long-term studies were conducted with fewer types of tasks. Holdings (1962) has taken the position that difficulty is not an especially useful concept for predicting transfer efficiency, and that the use of the concept of difficulty must give way to far more detailed or molecular analysis of the component skills involved. Nevertheless, we do have some leads on the transfer-difficulty issue. Deese (1958) has suggested that transfer may be greater from a difficult task provided that the difficult tasks contain all of the stimulus-response components of simpler tasks plus additional ones. On the other hand, transfer may be greater from an easy task if the easy task allows the learner to discover the relevant stimulus dimensions necessary for the solution of the complex task.

CHAPTER VI

Transfer and Stimulus Predifferentiation

WE NOTED IN CHAPTER I THAT PRACTICALLY ALL NEW learning is influenced in some fashion by previous learning. The purpose of this chapter is to examine the effects of a particular type of influence, preliminary experience with the stimulus aspects of a task, on transfer of learning. This preliminary experience with the stimulus aspects of a task is called *stimulus predifferentiation*. Let us consider the example given below.

In learning a new task such as driving a car, it is frequently reasonable to assume that the learner has had some prior experience with various stimulus components of the driving task. For example, the person may have spent some time in examining the various gauges on the dashboard so that he knows their location and purpose. He may have learned the location of the ignition, the light switch and brake release as well. In all likelihood, he can identify verbally a number of these stimulus components of the task even though he has never actually driven a car. Nevertheless, the fact that he has already learned to identify many of the important stimuli in driving will make the actual task of learning to drive considerably easier. This ease of learning to drive as a result of previous familiarity with the stimulus aspects of driving is an instance of stimulus predifferentiation.

The principle of stimulus predifferentiation is seen in a number of educational situations. The use of films and other audio-visual aids often serves to prepare the student to learn more readily complex skills and concepts. For example, students may be shown various parts of a microscope via filmstrips before they actually attempt to use a microscope. The assumption is made that this preliminary experience helps to "predifferentiate" the task so that whatever is learned subsequently will be learned with greater ease.

DEFINITION OF STIMULUS PREDIFFERENTIATION

In general, stimulus predifferentiation refers to the facilitation in learning a new stimulus-response task as a result of some type of preliminary experience or practice with the stimuli themselves. In the typical laboratory study of stimulus predifferentiation, subjects are given preliminary practice in attaching verbal labels, or names, to sets of stimuli and are then given a transfer task which requires them to make entirely different responses to the same stimuli. Usually, the transfer task requires motor responses such as pushing switches or levers; in this fashion the two sets of responses are quite different from each other, one verbal and the other motor. The basic features of this type of predifferentiation study are shown below:

Pretraining Task	*Transfer Task*
$S_0 - R_{verbal}$	$S_0 - R_{motor}$

It is reasoned that the ease of learning the transfer task—that is, of "hooking up" motor responses to the stimuli, occurs because the stimuli have become *predifferentiated* in the pretraining task. In other words, giving the various stimuli verbal labels has caused them to become less confusing or more "distinctive," thus making it easier to learn to attach new (motor) responses to them.

The essential features of a stimulus predifferentiation experiment are (1) that it provide some sort of preliminary practice or experience with the stimuli and (2) that the transfer task employ a set of responses different from those used in the pretraining task so that the positive transfer obtained *cannot* be attributed to any similarity between the two sets of responses. It is not necessary, however, for subjects to learn to make specific responses to the stimuli during pretraining; they may be required simply to "look at" or discriminate among the stimuli.

At this point you may ask in what way stimulus predifferentiation differs from the more conventional transfer study. In the usual transfer study in which the subject learns to attach new responses to the same stimuli, following the A–B, A–C paradigm, the responses are *qualitatively the same*. If they are verbal responses in the original task, they are also verbal responses in the transfer task. Although studies of stimulus predifferentiation do employ the A–B, A–C paradigm, the responses in the transfer task are *qualitatively different*. Studies of stimulus predifferentiation have the specific purpose of discovering the transfer effects of preliminary practice with the stimuli alone.

CATEGORIES OF STIMULUS PREDIFFERENTIATION

The previous section described one type of predifferentiation in which subjects practiced attaching verbal responses to stimuli during pretraining and then learned to make different motor responses to the *same* stimuli in the transfer task. This type of predifferentiation is known as *Relevant* S pretraining—that is, subjects are given pretraining with stimuli which are relevant (actually the same) to those used in the transfer task. There are several other types of stimulus predifferentiation which have been nicely classified by Arnoult (1957). His classification is based upon the various kinds of activities required of the subject during pretraining and is outlined in Table 1. Each type is illustrated with a hypothetical example for purposes of simplicity. The transfer task is the same in all instances and consists of making different motor responses of moving a control stick up in the presence of a red light and downward in the presence of a green light.

In the first type of pretraining, *Relevant S–R*, the stimuli in the pretraining task are the same as those in the transfer task, and the responses in the pretraining task are symbolic or "representative" of those in the transfer task. Presumably, learning to say "up" in the presence of a red light will make it easier to learn to move a control stick in the direction of up. This type of pretraining is not, strictly speaking, a type of stimulus predifferentiation since the responses in the training and transfer task are related to each other. Thus, any transfer obtained may result from the "relatedness" of the responses as well as any possible stimulus predifferentiation.

In the second type of pretraining, *Relevant S*, the stimuli in the two tasks are the same but the responses bear no symbolic relationship to each other. This type of pretraining is generally used in tests of hypotheses about stimulus predifferentiation (Gibson, 1940, Miller and Dollard, 1941). *Irrelevant S* pretraining requires that subjects make differential verbal responses to stimuli which are irrelevant to those in the transfer task. This type of training is most often used as a control for warm-up and learning to learn. *Attention training* requires subjects to "look at" or observe stimuli but not to label them in any way. A *No Pretraining* group is sometimes used as a control for the other conditions, but is generally unsatisfactory because it does not control for warm-up or learning to learn.

TABLE 1

Various Categories of Stimulus Predifferentiation *

Kind of Pretraining	Pretraining Task		Transfer Task	
	Stimulus	Verbal Responses	Stimulus	Motor Responses
Relevant S–R	Red light Green light	"Up" "Down"	Red light Green light	Up Down
Relevant S	Red light Green light	"Cow" "Horse"	Same as above	
Irrelevant S	Bright light Dim light	"Cow" "Horse"	Same as above	
Attention	Red light Green light	None None	Same as above	
No Pretraining	None		Same as above	

* Adapted from Arnoult (1957).

In all of the categories described by Arnoult, the transfer task consists of learning to make new responses to the stimuli: in other words, a discriminative *learning* task is used as a test of the effects of various types of predifferentiation. In addition, however, *perceptual* tasks have also been used which require that the subject discriminate or recognize stimuli rather than learn to make new responses in their presence. For example, following pretraining a subject may be given a recognition test in which he has to "pick out" from an array of similar stimuli the one or ones that he thought he experienced during pretraining.

EFFECTS OF VARIOUS TYPES OF PRETRAINING ON TRANSFER

The effects of various types of pretraining on transfer are reasonably well established and clear. To begin with, studies which have used Relevant S–R pretraining have uniformly shown equal or greater positive transfer as compared with other kinds of pretraining. This is an understandable effect since not only do the stimuli become predifferentiated but the responses in the transfer task are easier to learn because of practice on relevant symbolic features during pretraining.

Relevant S pretraining has also been shown to produce significant amounts of positive transfer in a large number of experiments (for example, Battig, 1956, Cantor, 1953, Ellis and Muller [6],[1] Gagné and Baker, 1950, Goss, 1953, Goss and Greenfeld, 1958, McAllister, 1953, Norcross and Spiker, 1958, Vanderplas, Sanderson, and Vanderplas, 1964). In general, these studies have required that subjects practice a preliminary task in which they learn to give distinctive verbal labels to stimuli and then perform on a transfer task in which they learn to make differential motor responses to the same stimuli. The ease with which subjects learn the transfer task is interpreted as being due to the preliminary experience with the stimuli that presumably makes them less confusing. Exactly how the stimuli become less confusing or more distinctive and precisely what mechanisms are involved is a subject of theoretical controversy, and several alternative hypotheses have been offered to account for this event (Gibson, 1963, Gibson and Gibson, 1955, Hake and Ericksen, 1955, Miller and Dollard, 1941, Postman, 1955, Vanderplas, 1963). Regardless of theoretical differences in interpretation, however, the facts regarding Relevant S pretraining are quite clear.

A study by Gagné and Baker (1950) will illustrate the effects of Relevant S pretraining. One group of subjects received preliminary experience in learning to associate letters of the alphabet to different lights whereas another group received no preliminary pretraining. Both groups were then given a transfer task which required them to learn to press a particular switch in the presence of each of the

[1] Bracketed numbers refer to readings in Part Two.

lights. Subjects given practice in associating letters to lights were superior in learning the transfer task to those given no pretraining. The results were interpreted as indicating that pretraining served to make the stimuli less confusing—that is, to reduce the amount of stimulus generalization among the stimuli. Unfortunately, the results were probably confounded with learning to learn and warm-up since no controls for these effects were employed.

A more elaborate study by Goss and Greenfeld (1958) attempted to examine in greater detail the various conditions influencing transfer of predifferentiation. In their study, several different types of pretraining were given along with several degrees of practice on the pretraining task plus a control group which received no pretraining. The pretraining portion of the study required subjects to engage in one of several tasks with stimuli consisting of four lights of varying intensity. The various pretraining tasks included such activities as attaching familiar relevant labels to the stimuli—that is, learning to call them *very bright, bright, dull,* and *very dull,* labeling the stimuli with nonsense syllables, and having the subjects supply their own labels. Besides the three different verbal labeling conditions, other conditions were given which involved various combinations as follows: looking at the stimuli; looking at and discriminating among the stimuli; and looking, discriminating and naming overtly or covertly.

Following pretraining, the subjects were given a transfer task in which they had to learn to push a lever in a different direction for each of the four lights. Although detailed results are reported, the basic findings of the study revealed that subjects given the various verbal labeling tasks were superior on the transfer task to those given instructions which involved various combinations of looking at, discriminating, and naming overtly or covertly. In addition, all conditions led to superior transfer when compared with groups who only saw the stimuli. The pronounced superiority of the various verbal labeling groups over the "seeing" group was quite striking. Goss and Greenfeld viewed their results as being consistent with the hypothesis of response produced cues—namely, that attaching verbal responses to the stimuli generated additional cues which served to make them more distinctive.

Battig (1956) and Vanderplas *et al.* (1964) also have shown that transfer from verbal pretraining to a motor task is dependent on additional conditions. Battig showed that the degree of transfer from verbal pretraining to a motor task depends upon the complexity of the task; the amount of transfer decreased as complexity of the motor task increased. In an elaborate study varying *both* type of pretraining and type of transfer task, Vanderplas *et al.* showed that the amount of transfer to perceptual and perceptual-motor tasks depended upon the gross similarity between the pretraining and transfer tasks.

THE INFLUENCE OF LABELING: AN ILLUSTRATION

So far we have seen that learning to attach different labels to similar stimuli makes it possible to respond to these stimuli differently. Indeed, verbal labels serve to mediate or to facilitate the learning of new and different responses to stimuli in a number of everyday situations. Let us consider a fairly common situation among college students. Suppose you are in a quandary about asking two girls, Jean and Nancy, for a date to attend a campus dance. You have seen them on campus, find them physically attractive, but otherwise know almost nothing about them. You decide to inquire among friends, and one of them tells you that Jean is a rather cold and distant person who is difficult to get to know. Nancy, on the other hand, is described as warm, fun-loving and a good conversationalist. In all likelihood, other things being equal, you will ask Nancy for the date. In this instance, the descriptive labels given Nancy make it easy for you to make additional responses toward her, namely, asking her for a date. According to one theory, that of *acquired-distinctiveness of cues*, the distinctive verbal labels have become "cues" for making additional responses.

A complementary process has also been proposed which is called *acquired equivalence of cues*. Suppose you are interested in dating a particular girl who is a member of a specific sorority. The members of this sorority are held in low esteem and, in general, have a poor reputation on campus. Even though this particular girl may be extremely desirable, you may be reluctant to date her if you are aware of her sorority's reputation. In this instance, a class of labels has, as we say, generalized to all members of the group and there is a tendency, therefore, to treat all members somewhat similarly.

This phenomenon of acquired equivalence seems to be part of the basis of racial and ethnic prejudice. Everyday instances of situations in which a person was well liked and accepted by a group until it was discovered that he was "Jewish" are numerous. In other words, the label "Jew" can serve to mediate entirely new reactions from others even though the person himself has not changed.

Role of the Transfer Task Itself

Not all experiments have shown positive transfer effects resulting from labeling practice (for example, Arnoult, 1953, and 1956, Ellis, Bessemer, Devine, and Trafton, 1962, Robinson, 1955). In these studies the transfer task was a perceptual rather than a learning task, a distinction which can be illustrated by examining Robinson's study.

Robinson gave independent groups of subjects several types of pretraining with stimuli, which consisted of photographs of ten different fingerprints. One group of subjects learned to attach distinctive names to the fingerprints, gangsters' nicknames; another group learned one name, "cops," for half the stimuli, and "robbers" for the remaining half; a third group was given practice in making "same-different" judgments when shown successive pairs of fingerprints; a control group received no pretraining. On the transfer task, the subjects were shown the same ten fingerprints plus additional ones and were required to make "same-different" judgments when shown successive pairs of fingerprints.

The findings were as follows: (1) all pretraining groups were superior to the control in the accuracy of their judgments, and (2) *no differences* were found among any of the pretraining groups. In other words, preliminary practice in labeling the fingerprints with distinctive verbal labels did not increase the discriminability of the stimuli over that improvement resulting from pretraining without labels.

Can the failure to obtain positive effects from labeling be due to the transfer task itself? In other words, are the differences a result of the use of *learning* tasks in one set of experiments and *perceptual* tasks in another? Ellis and Muller [6] and Vanderplas *et al.* (1964) reasoned that this was the case and obtained substantial evidence to support their position. Vanderplas (1963) had earlier noted that when perceptual transfer tasks were used, such as discrimination or recognition tasks, distinctive verbal labeling of stimuli yielded no more transfer than did preliminary instructions to observe or discriminate the stimuli. Nevertheless, gross comparisons of the various studies using the two types of transfer tasks were not themselves sufficient since none of them had employed identical types of pretraining, the same stimuli, labels, and so on.

In order to directly compare the two types of transfer tasks Ellis and Muller [6] conducted an experiment in which subjects were given identical pretraining and then tested either on a learning or a perceptual transfer task. They gave subjects a pretraining task using random shapes, examples of which are shown in Figure 2.

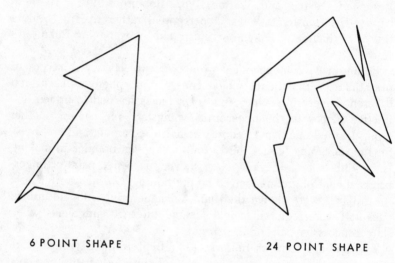

6 POINT SHAPE   24 POINT SHAPE

FIGURE 2. Examples of random shapes. (Adapted from Vanderplas & Garvin, 1959.)

Subjects were given practice in either labeling simple (6-point) random shapes with distinctive relevant labels which were descriptive of the shapes, or they were instructed only to observe and discriminate the shapes. Subjects were given an equal amount of practice for the labeling and observation conditions for either two, four, eight, or sixteen trials. Following pretraining, some subjects were given a recognition test in which they were shown sets of similar random shapes, some they had seen and some they had not seen, and were asked if they recognized any of the shapes as ones they had experienced before. Other subjects were given a learning task which required them to learn to press one of eight switches for each of the eight shapes experienced during pretraining.

The basic results of the study are seen in Figure 3. The labeling group is somewhat inferior to the observation group in terms of the number of correct recognitions they make. Certainly, the labeling does not aid subsequent recognition when compared with a group given observation practice alone, even though both groups do improve with practice. On the other hand, the labeling group is superior to the observation group in learning to attach motor responses to the stimuli. Quite clearly, the effect of labeling can depend upon the nature of the transfer task. Labeling may help if the transfer

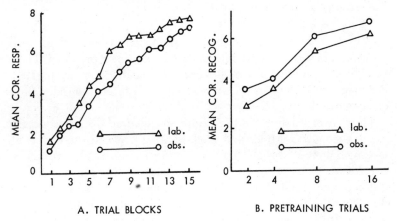

A. TRIAL BLOCKS   B. PRETRAINING TRIALS

FIGURE 3. Comparison of the effects of labeling and observation on transfer to two different types of tasks. *A*, shows transfer to an instrumental *learning task* (mean correct motor-switching responses to stimuli as a function of type of pretraining). *B*, shows transfer to a *perceptual task* (mean correct recognition of stimuli as a function of type of pretraining). (Adapted from Ellis & Muller, 1964.)

task requires subjects to make new responses to the stimuli and may not help if the task is one of recognition.

It is not possible, however, to generalize that the effect of verbal labeling is to facilitate only learning and not perception since Ellis and Muller found some evidence for improved shape recognition following labeling practice when the shapes were complex (twenty-four-point shapes). Nevertheless, the findings with respect to simple shapes are systematic with respect to the distinction between perceptual and learning tasks.

Why this difference between the two types of transfer tasks? Why, in general, does labeling of stimuli facilitate a subsequent task when it involves making new responses to the stimuli and have little or no effect when the task is one of recognition or discrimination? No completely adequate explanation exists. It would appear, perhaps, that cues which are generated as a result of labeling may be non-functional in the perceptual task—that is, unnecessary for improving perception. In the learning task, the cues generated from labeling appear to be used, perhaps serving as conditioned stimuli in the acquisition of new responses (Goss, 1955, Miller and Dollard, 1941).

Theories of Stimulus Predifferentiation

A variety of theories to account for the positive transfer effects resulting from stimulus predifferentiation have been proposed. These have been described in several sources (Arnoult, 1957, Bevan, 1961, Postman, 1963, Vanderplas, 1958). We shall briefly consider three of these hypotheses.

The first of these is the hypothesis of *acquired distinctiveness of cues* (Goss, 1955, Miller and Dollard, 1941), which states that attaching different verbal labels to similar stimuli tends to increase the "distinctiveness" of the stimuli as a result of the addition of different response-produced cues. The function of a label is to produce additional cues which in turn make similar stimuli more distinctive. In this theory, "distinctiveness" is treated as an intervening variable and is inferred from the ease in which one attaches new instrumental responses to stimuli following labeling practice, or in the improvement in recognition or discrimination following labeling practice. Miller and Dollard usually refer to instances that involve instrumental responses although their definition implies some sort of change in perceptual responses as well. Attempts to test this hypothesis have yielded somewhat contradictory results. In general, attempts to test this hypothesis with instrumental transfer tasks— that is, those which require learning to make new responses to the stimuli have yielded results which have been interpreted in favor of the hypothesis; in contrast, attempts to test the hypothesis using perceptual tasks have yielded results which have not supported the hypothesis. This is an oversimplification of the findings and more rigorous tests of this hypothesis will require better specification of both the stimulus and response conditions as well as the development of more adequate conceptualizations about the events involved (Arnoult, 1957).

Ellis and Muller [6] have raised an additional question as to whether it is entirely appropriate to interpret the positive transfer effects resulting from Relevant S training as being due to the increased distinctiveness of the stimuli alone. Even though the responses in the training and transfer task are qualitatively different, they have suggested that learning how to make *identifying* (naming) *responses* in the training task may aid in the making of new identifying responses in the transfer task even though the responses are qualitatively different. In other words, Relevant S training may, in fact, produce two effects, one being to increase the distinctiveness of the stimuli and the other to facilitate a learning-how-to-learn process in which subjects acquire skill in making identifying responses. They further point out that if, indeed, labeling practice does increase the "distinctiveness" of stimuli, that such increase ought to be reflected in a perceptual task such as recognition as well as in a learning task which requires differential motor responses.

Gibson (1940) has proposed an hypothesis to account for the findings of stimulus predifferentiation in terms of the *reduction of intralist generalization*. Accordingly, the effect of pretraining is to reduce the amount of stimulus generalization among the stimulus items in a list. As the amount of generalization among stimuli is reduced, the amount of positive transfer in learning a new task is increased. According to Arnoult, this hypothesis is operationally equivalent to the distinctiveness of cues hypothesis; however, Gibson does *not* say that generalization is reduced as a result of distinctive response-produced cues being added to the stimuli. In other words, both theories predict similar effects, but for somewhat different reasons. This distinction is amplified by Gibson and Gibson (1955), who subsequently proposed that stimuli become perceptually more distinctive not as a result of some "enrichment" process, but as a result of "differentiation." Individuals learn to distinguish various components which already exist in the stimulus, that is, they learn to respond to various stimuli not previously responded to rather than enriching the stimulus through the addition of response-produced cues. Although these two hypotheses have received considerable attention in recent experiments, it is too early to decide on their respective merits.

Hake and Ericksen (1955) have suggested that the role of verbal labels in the pretraining task is to force the subject to attend to various cues. Such a view implies that the label helps the subject to

select certain features of the stimuli and that it is the general labeling process rather than the specific features of the labels themselves
which is important. The *Attention to Cues* hypothesis has also been
suggested by Robinson (1955), although the hypothesis has been
somewhat difficult to test.

In summary, no single theory appears adequate in accounting for
the empirical phenomenon of stimulus predifferentiation. Part of this
difficulty may lie in inadequate or incomplete conceptualization of
the events involved. In addition, failure to specify precisely the
meaning of various constructs employed in the theories may also
account for some of their difficulty. It is conceivable that all of the
proposed theories may be adequate for limited sets of data and that
a more comprehensive theory will emerge as a result of better integration of the theories. Gibson (1963) has recently suggested that
further progress in resolving these theoretical issues will result only
after more creative handling of the hypotheses and after more careful consideration of the experimental designs employed.

CHAPTER VII

Transfer and the Educational Process

SO FAR WE HAVE DESCRIBED A NUMBER OF CONDITIONS known to influence transfer of learning and indicated several theoretical problems of transfer. We now turn our attention to the role of transfer in the educational process and examine those factors which are relevant and applicable to classroom learning activities. At this point, it is significant to note that early studies of transfer of learning, indeed much of human learning, were first conducted in the classroom as distinct from the laboratory in an attempt to better understand the teaching-learning process; in addition, many of these studies were orientated towards examining conceptions of transfer which had direct relevance to educational practices.

Later, around 1930, increasing effort was placed upon laboratory studies of learning that had as one of their main goals the attempt to develop *laws* of behavior. It was felt that a science of human behavior could be best developed through carefully controlled laboratory studies of the learning process. Certainly, classroom studies of learning are important, but it was argued that the complexity of the classroom environment made it difficult to discover fundamental laws of learning.

Although the necessity for carefully-controlled and systematic studies of the learning process has never been doubted by most psychologists (for example, Spence, 1956), rumblings were heard which suggested that all was not well. A number of educators and training specialists began to ask psychologists for help in problems associated with learning. Increasingly, psychologists faced the question: "What is there in the psychology of learning which is useful and applicable to educational problems?" It was possible for psychologists to take at least three rather distinct positions on this issue: (1) one alternative was to reject the plea of the educator by either showing little interest in his problems or by arguing that psychology was not ready to help because it didn't have adequately-developed laws of behavior; (2) a second approach of the psychologist was to take stock of his facts, principles, and theories and to make recommendations, in some cases quite tentative, about applying principles of learning to educational problems and to make suggestions about potentially fruitful areas for further research; (3) a third alternative was for the psychologist to tackle directly the problems of education by becoming an educator himself.

This chapter reflects the view that, for the present, the second option appears most fruitful. Here the role of the psychologist is to help clarify what is known about the learning process and to make suggestions about specific practices based on his knowledge of this process. This position implies that some psychologists will serve the function of translating knowledge of learning into useful principles for educational practice; in other words, an important task for at least *some* learning psychologists is to bridge the gap between the events of the laboratory and those of educational practice. A more detailed account of points of view on the relationship between learning theory and educational practice may be seen in a recent symposium by Spence, Melton, and Underwood (1959).

EARLY THEORIES OF TRANSFER AND EDUCATION

A prominent and long-held view by many educators was the doctrine of *formal discipline*. This view contended that the "mind" was composed of several faculties such as reasoning, memory, judgment, and attention, and that these faculties could be trained, improved, and strengthened through the study of certain kinds of subject matter. An important objective of education was the study of specific subjects in order that such study would "discipline" the "mind." Studies such as mathematics and Latin were regarded as extremely important because they strengthened reasoning and memory. Geometry was regarded as an especially good subject for improving logical reasoning and ancient languages as important because they sharpened the student's memory ability.

Around the turn of the century this doctrine came under experimental attack. An early study by Thorndike and Woodworth (1901) critically examined the notion of formal discipline and failed to find any substantial evidence in support of it. For about twenty-five years following their classic study, a number of investigations were conducted with little or no support for the doctrine resulting. As a result, educators gradually abandoned this viewpoint and, in turn, modified some of their teaching goals. For example, students were no longer taught mathematics because of presumed strengthening of reasoning ability, but were taught mathematics because it was an important subject matter in its own right.

The theory of formal discipline tended to assume that transfer was widespread and fairly automatic. As a result of attack upon it, however, a new view emerged that regarded transfer as much more limited in scope. As indicated, the challenge to formal discipline came from Thorndike and Woodworth (1901) who, on the basis of their investigations, concluded that transfer of training was limited to those situations in which the two tasks contained "identical elements." The theory of *identical elements* contended that training in one kind of activity would transfer to another as long as certain features such as aims, methods, and approaches were identical in the two tasks. Whereas formal discipline argued that transfer was very general and widespread, the theory of identical elements viewed transfer as more restricted in scope. Thus, hope for widespread transfer decreased and more emphasis was placed upon direct training of desired educational objectives.

Critics of the identical elements theory appeared and argued that it was too specific, and that transfer was not limited to situations containing identical elements. The concept of element itself was also under attack with some arguing that complex experiences could not be reduced to simple elements. There is reason to think, however, that Thorndike and Woodworth had a much broader conception of "elements" than some of their critics assumed. For example, these elements included such things as general principles and attitudes as well as more specific aspects of the tasks.

In addition, the identical elements theory came under attack as a result of studies by Judd (1908) and his colleagues. Judd argued that the important condition for transfer was that the student be able to abstract general rules or principles for himself. He called this a *theory of generalization,* which meant that a student was able to "generalize" his experiences from one situation and apply them to another. Thus, in order to teach for transfer, emphasis should be placed on getting the student to think about those features of the problem that might be generalized to new situations. The generalization theory had the advantage of at least recognizing that transfer was not an automatic process, and that, if one wanted students to transfer, they must be given practice in transfer. Unfortunately, as Schulz (1960) has noted, it is not enough to exhort a teacher to "teach for transfer." Clearly, in order to teach for transfer we must have a fairly explicit understanding of the criterion behaviors to be exhibited by students and the kinds of conditions which will insure the development of these behaviors. In other words, we must have a fairly explicit understanding of the *variables* known to influence transfer before a technology of application can develop.

A CONTEMPORARY APPROACH TO TRANSFER

These existing theories of transfer, perhaps better described as *points of view* rather than theories in the more formal sense, serve as focal points for viewing educational issues. The theories are all stated in rather general language, thus making them somewhat difficult to test in a rigorous fashion. Indeed, for this reason, Osgood (1953) has indicated that one cannot be sure that the old doctrine of formal discipline is invalid. Quite conceivably, there is some validity to all of these points of view and that the issue is to determine the conditions under which each might be useful. Nevertheless, the author contends that it is more fruitful for education to take stock of the known variables which do influence transfer rather than to debate more speculative points of view. This approach is neither antitheoretical nor atheoretical as such but contends that in order to apply principles of transfer in the classroom, the teacher should have a good understanding of the basic factors which do influence transfer. So far, we have examined a number of important factors in transfer and this chapter will examine several additional factors which have been studied in the context of classroom teaching.

LEARNER CHARACTERISTICS AND TRANSFER

Several learner characteristics are also known to influence transfer. These characteristics include such factors as intelligence of the learner and motivational factors including anxiety. In general, it is difficult to make over-all generalizations about many of these factors, partly because not enough information is known about them and partly because these factors appear to be important in some learning situations and not in others.

It would be quite surprising if the intelligent student were not the more successful in transferring his knowledge and skills to new situations. Many studies which have investigated the role of intelligence do find that the more intelligent students show greater transfer (for example, Craig, 1953, Werner, 1930); however, this generalization has not been tested over a wide variety of tasks and school subjects. A typical finding is that of Werner (1930), who found that students above average in intelligence were able to profit from foreign language studies when tested on their ability in English whereas students of average intelligence were not. A reasonable interpretation of this and similar findings is that brighter students tend to seek out relationships and are more likely to have a set for transfer than do the less bright students.

To the extent that motivational variables influence learning, they are also likely to influence transfer. If a student is poorly motivated he will tend to learn less, thus reducing the chance of transfer to new learning situations. One motivational variable, anxiety, has been extensively studied in recent years (Spence, 1964), and some fairly reliable generalizations about its effect on learning are evident. One generalization which has significant implications for classroom teaching is that anxiety appears to facilitate performance in relatively simple types of learning, such as conditioning, but interferes with performance in more complex learning tasks. Certainly, it is reasonable to assume that anxiety will interfere with most classroom learning which generally consists of tasks of a fairly complex nature.

In the studies of Spence (1964) and his colleagues, anxiety is viewed as a motivational variable that increases the probability of various responses being made in a learning situation. If there is only one or at best a few responses which are possible, then anxiety tends to increase the likelihood of a correct response. This will occur simply because there are so few response alternatives. On the other hand, if many responses are possible, which is the case with more complex learning tasks, then anxiety tends to increase the likelihood of one or more incorrect or competing responses. This theoretical conception of anxiety has been shown to handle the laboratory studies of learning quite well and appears to be applicable to a study of classroom learning reported by Gaier (1952).

Specifically, Gaier was interested in finding out the effects of anxiety on thinking and on subsequent test performance of students in a social science course. In this study he distinguished between two kinds of tests: those requiring primarily the factual recall of material and those emphasizing more complex behaviors such as analysis, synthesis, and application of principles. In general, his findings were in agreement with those of the later laboratory studies regarding the interaction between anxiety and task complexity. For example, he found that students of high anxiety performed somewhat better than those of low anxiety on tests emphasizing memory for facts. In contrast, students of low anxiety performed significantly better on tests that required more complex behaviors such as synthesis and application. An interesting finding about the students' thought processes in class was that the anxious students spent significantly more time in thinking about concrete objects in the class such as the instructor's dress or a crack in the wall than on aspects of the lecture. Gaier's findings, in general, are consistent with the notion that heightened anxiety lowers the threshold for additional responses which are irrelevant to and compete with the desirable intellectual responses necessary for adequate classroom performance.

TRANSFER AND PROBLEM SOLVING

One of the significant objectives of education is that of teaching students effective ways of solving problems. Sometimes this objective is cast in the form of teaching students to "think" or to "reason for themselves." Regardless of the manner in which this objective is stated, it clearly implies that the conditions under which a student learns will govern to some extent his subsequent skill in solving problems. The methods, approaches, and attitudes that are present during learning will affect in some way the student's later performance, that is, these conditions have the potentiality of producing transfer of some magnitude and direction.

Traditionally, the topic of problem solving has been treated separately from that of transfer (Duncan, 1959). A recent analysis, however, has shown that many studies of problem solving can, in fact, be treated as studies of transfer (Schulz, 1960). Generally, studies of problem solving involve two phases: some type of preliminary activity in which the learner practices a task under specified conditions and a subsequent criterion task which is related to the preliminary activity. Usually, the criterion task is high on the discovery dimension that is, the learner has to discover appropriate responses for solving the problem. In addition, the preliminary task is frequently designed so that it will interfere with efficient problem solving activity. Thus, the usual study of problem solving takes the form of a negative transfer design although there is nothing about problem solving *per se* which requires this feature.

Both Duncan (1959) and Marx (1958) have made the plea that problem solving especially needs research orientated toward determining functional relationships between antecedent conditions, such as conditions of practice, and various measures of performance. This view is quite consistent with that expressed at the beginning of this chapter. At present, the field of problem solving is poorly integrated and with the exception of a few areas (for example, Maltzman, 1955), it lacks systematic and intensive investigations of a long-term nature. Nevertheless, there are several important generalizations which can be made about transfer effects in problem solving and these will be described in this section. This discussion is naturally selective and we will confine ourselves to three types of factors studied: (1) variations in the mode of problem solving—that is, meaningful versus "rote" approaches; (2) the effects of group participation; and (3) the variety of tasks experienced during training. These factors were selected because of their relevance to classroom practices.

The effect of different methods of first-task practice on transfer to a second task has been studied by Hilgard, Irvine, and Whipple (1953). College students were first required to learn solutions to card trick problems in which they had to arrange a deck of cards so that when dealt the cards would appear in a certain order. One group was shown a formula by which the ordering could be reasoned out or "understood," and a comparable group simply memorized the solutions. Although the "understanding" group took more time to learn the solutions, they performed significantly better when they were required to learn new but related problems. In other words, transfer to the new task was superior when the students understood the principle involved.

Another problem of concern to education is the issue of transfer effects from group participation. Although a number of investigations have shown that group problem solving activity is superior to that of individual activity (for example, Taylor and Faust, 1952), the assumption that skills acquired in group activity will necessarily transfer to the individual situation is unwarranted. In a recent study, Hudgins [7] [1] addressed himself to this problem by noting that this assumption appeared to be widely accepted despite the fact that little evidence on the issue was available. Using fifth-grade students, Hudgins first gave them three consecutive days of practice in solving arithmetic problems, half working in groups of four students and half working alone. During this phase, he found that the students working in groups solved consistently more problems than did those working as individuals. On the second or transfer phase, all students continued to solve arithmetic problems, but on an individual basis. Here he found no difference in performance between those who had earlier worked as members of a group and those who had worked as individuals. In other words, there was no evidence for any transfer as a function of working with a group despite the fact that groups were superior in the original task.

Hudgins' findings do not, of course, mean that there are no possible advantages from group activity. Conceivably, desirable social skills and other behaviors are acquired and do transfer to new situations. His findings do indicate that considerably more research on this factor needs to be made before general conclusions are drawn about the transfer effects of group activity. Perhaps three days of practice was not sufficient to provide opportunity for group experiences to transfer. On theoretical grounds, it would appear that the effect of working with a group might transfer to an individual situation, provided that students were reinforced for group activity as such. In other words, the benefits of mutual exchange of information and skills could conceivably transfer if direct emphasis were placed upon these kinds of events. This might involve instructing students to assist each other in solving problems in a rather definite fashion.

The third factor to be considered concerns the role of task variety

[1] Bracketed numbers refer to readings in Part Two.

on the transfer of problem-solving skills. We noted in Chapter V that there was evidence to indicate that greater task variety led to enhanced positive transfer in studies that involved paired-associate learning tasks. The evidence suggests that a similar relationship holds with problem-solving tasks as well. In a relatively simple study, Morrisett and Hovland (1959) have demonstrated the importance of task variety in human problem solving. The most significant finding of their study was that preliminary training that gives the learner opportunity to both fully learn a particular type of problem as well as experience several types of problems yields maximum transfer. A high degree of original learning is important in order to strengthen the correct response tendencies, and practice with a variety of tasks provides the learner with opportunity to discriminate between relevant and irrelevant cues.

TRANSFER AND PROGRAMED INSTRUCTION

A development of considerable interest in recent years is that of programed instruction and teaching machines. Briefly, programed instruction is a procedure for teaching various topics by requiring students to respond to well-developed sequences of problems that have been organized on the basis of learner responses. The student reads a statement and is usually required to answer some question about the statement. The material is developed in a logical and orderly fashion so that the student gradually acquires understanding of more complex concepts. The chief features of programed instruction are as follows: (1) the learner responds in an active fashion to the material; (2) the learner receives immediate confirmation of the correctness of his response; (3) the learner proceeds at his own pace; and (4) the learner studies a program that has been carefully designed and tested in order to insure maximum learning. It is not our purpose to describe the considerable details of programed instruction because numerous accounts of this educational technology have been given (for example, Lumsdaine and Glaser, 1960, Skinner, 1958, Stolurow, 1961). Rather, our purpose is to note some implications of programed instruction for transfer.

An interesting feature about programed instruction is that programs are generally developed with the purpose of maximizing student achievement, usually defined in terms of performance on some test given upon completion of the program, or in terms of the difference between pretest and posttest scores (Ellis, 1964). In other words, the success of the program is largely defined by the amount of achievement it produces. This approach is certainly not unreasonable and does have the advantage of establishing relatively objective criteria for evaluating programs. Nevertheless, this emphasis tends either to ignore or to leave unanswered the issue of transfer of knowledge and skills that presumably result from practice with programed instructional materials. Indeed, with the exception of a few studies (for example, Gagné and Dick, 1962, Taber and Glaser, 1962), research in programed instruction has largely ignored the issue of transfer.

What appears to be especially desirable are studies that yield evidence that not only does the program teach, but that students can transfer their learning beyond the immediate context of the program. Such studies would be directed toward discovering features of programs that produce considerable transfer. At present, Stolurow (1963) and his colleagues are engaged in intensive investigations of this type in which they are studying the form, sequence and size of step, where step refers to a unit of material in the program, as possible factors influencing transfer with the objective of being able to specify guide line for writers of programs.

TEACHING FOR TRANSFER

We are now ready to specific a few guidelines for teaching so that what is taught is more likely to transfer to new learning situations. We have examined a large number of factors influencing transfer and will now illustrate how several of these might be applied to classroom teaching. Undoubtedly, any attempt to make an exhaustive list of illustrations would leave us with an unwieldy list, so the present list is to be regarded as only suggestive of a number of possibilities.

1. *Maximize the similarity between teaching and the ultimate testing situation.* A teacher who hopes to induce much transfer must attempt to teach under conditions which are at least somewhat similar to the ultimate testing situation. The attempt to maximize similarity can be made in several ways, although it should be realized that this is an idealized goal and many events may make it difficult to achieve. A good way to begin to apply this principle is to first ask yourself what it is that you want your students to know—that is,

what you think is important—and to begin by both teaching and testing for these consequences. Obviously, to teach for one thing and test for another is to invite difficulty.

Ways of implementing this principle are numerous. For example, in teaching students to solve arithmetic problems, direct practice in solving "word problems" can be given rather than simply expecting students to solve word problems when they first face them. Similarly, students can be familiarized with various aspects of a complex task by viewing it as it exists in a "real" situation via educational films or television. Also, if a typist is likely to work in a pool of typists, then somewhere during her training she should be given practice in typing among other typists in order to experience conditions of noise and interruption as well as other conditions. In general, the application of this principle requires that somewhere during the student's educational sequence, he be given practice in an environment which contains many of those factors which will exist in the ultimate working environment.

2. *Provide adequate experience with the original task.* We have seen that extensive practice on the original task increases the likelihood of positive transfer to a subsequent task, whereas more limited practice may yield no transfer or even negative transfer. Related to this point is the work of Harlow [3], which implies that very thorough practice should be given in the early stage of developing new skills and concepts. Later on, such thoroughness may not be required. It is difficult, of course, in a given learning situation to specify precisely how much practice is desirable on a specific task; nevertheless, a good rule of thumb would be to have students receive as much practice as is feasible considering the restraints imposed by the various activities in a modern classroom. In addition, the teacher is somewhat free to be selective in the degree of emphasis placed on various topics. Perhaps greater emphasis could be placed on those topics that are known to be necessary for the mastery of subsequent course work. For example, if a student is to pursue additional work in mathematics, it is necessary that he understand the more elementary aspects of the subject. Other subject matter, in contrast, which does not have this sequential dependency, may not require as much practice.

3. *Provide for a variety of examples when teaching concepts and principles.* Studies in concept formation and in problem solving indicate that stimulus variety is an important factor leading to posi-

tive transfer. Several examples of a concept serve to strengthen the student's understanding so that he is more likely to see the applicability of a concept in a new situation. In addition, the students should be given examples of instances which do not represent the concept, particularly examples which are likely to be confused by the student. Distinctions, particularly among vague concepts, are more likely to be clarified with many examples.

4. *Label or identify important features of a task*. We have seen in studies of stimulus predifferentiation that the labeling of important features of a task aids in our subsequent learning of the task. Labeling helps us to distinguish important features of a task, although we are not entirely sure whether this is due merely to increased attention given to these features or whether it is due to the label itself. An illustration of this principle can be seen in teaching of young children to distinguish between the letters *b* and *d*, a fairly common source of difficulty. One way of helping them is to show them similar words such as *big* and *dig* and help them to identify the crucial difference between the two words.

5. *Make sure that general principles are understood before expecting much transfer*. If we expect students to show much transfer in course work that involves general principles, we must be reasonably sure that the principles are thoroughly understood. In the course of teaching a particular concept or principle, such as how to solve quadratic equations, the teacher can check periodically to discover if students do understand certain operations. In addition, the problem can be presented several ways and students may be required to discover errors in solutions and correct them. Sometimes the teacher can check for the students' understanding by presenting a problem in a novel context, such as using new symbols in the same formula.

SOME PRINCIPLES OF TRANSFER

It is appropriate at the end of this chapter to summarize some of the major empirical principles of transfer. The principles are stated in rather general fashion and detailed qualifications have been largely avoided for purposes of simplicity. The statements can serve as general guidelines for educational practice and as a point of departure for future research.

1. *Over-all task similarity*. Transfer of training is greatest when

the training conditions are highly similar to those of the ultimate testing conditions.

2. *Stimulus similarity.* When a task requires the learner to make the same response to new but similar stimuli, positive transfer increases with increasing stimulus similarity.

3. *Response similarity.* When a task requires the learner to make a new or different response to the same stimuli, transfer tends to be negative and increases as the responses become less similar.

   (a) Under conditions of high response similarity, this condition can produce positive transfer.

   (b) Also, it is usually more difficult under this condition to obtain negative transfer in verbal learning than it is in motor skills learning.

4. *Joint stimulus-response variation.* If the responses in the transfer task are different from those in the original task, then the greater the similarity of stimuli, the less the positive transfer.

5. *Learning-to-learn.* Cumulative practice in learning a series of related tasks or problems leads to increased facility in learning how to learn.

6. *Early-task learning.* Transfer is maximized if greater effort is spent in mastering the early of a series of related tasks.

7. *Insight.* Insight, defined behaviorally as the rapid solution of problems, appears to develop as a result of extensive practice in solving similar or related classes of problems.

8. *Warm-up.* Warm-up is the pronounced but temporary facilitating effect resulting from practice in some activity prior to learning the transfer task.

9. *Time interval between tasks.* Performance on the second task is minimally determined by the time elapsing between original and transfer tasks, as long as the transfer task involves little memory for specific aspects of the original task.

10. *Mediated transfer.* Transfer can occur as a result of mediation due to the network of associative linkages between tasks.

11. *Bilateral transfer.* Positive transfer can be obtained as a result of practice with one limb to its analogous limb.

12. *Task or stimulus variety.* In general, variety of tasks, or of their stimulus components, during original learning increases the amount of positive transfer obtained.

13. *Amount of practice on the original task.* The greater the amount of practice on the original task, the greater the likelihood of

positive transfer; negative transfer is likely to occur following only limited practice on the original task.

14. *Task characteristics.*   No clear-cut generalizations about the role of task characteristics such as difficulty or complexity appear evident.

15. *Stimulus predifferentiation.*   Relevant S pretraining leads to positive transfer when the transfer task involves learning; evidence for relevant S effects on perceptual tasks is negative or at best dubious.

16. *Understanding and transfer.*   Transfer is greater if the learner understands the general rules or principles which are appropriate in solving new problems.

17. *Group learning.*   There is no evidence for the automatic transfer of problem solving skills from a group to an individual situation.

CHAPTER VIII

Theoretical Developments in Transfer

IN THIS CHAPTER WE SHALL DESCRIBE SOME OF THE theoretical developments in transfer of learning. Up to this point, no attempt has been made to treat theory extensively, with the exception of theories of stimulus predifferentiation. A major reason for this has been the relatively limited development of theories of transfer. Indeed, a problem in transfer until recently has been the lack of systematic theory that would serve both to organize the diverse empirical findings and to predict new relationships. Certainly, a number of functional relationships have been established; however, they have not always been easily integrated within the framework of systematic theory. Where theory has developed, it has with few exceptions been largely of the functionalist variety, which is characterized by its close adherence to the data and its avoidance of extensive speculation. Finally, and unfortunately, some researchers in transfer have been content to establish functional relationships between measures of transfer and various conditions which influence transfer without great concern for theoretical interpretation of such relationships.

Currently, there are at least six areas of investigation in transfer that are showing considerable progress in the development of theory or conceptual models. These areas include: (1) mediation, (2) stimulus predifferentiation, (3) transposition, (4) paired-associate verbal learning, (5) learning set theory, and (6) mathematical models. Developments in the first two areas have been described earlier and the remaining portion of this chapter will be devoted to describing representative efforts in the latter four areas.

TRANSPOSITION

There is one major exception to the generalizations outlined in the opening paragraph. This exception is reflected in the longstanding controversy regarding the nature of discrimination learning. This controversy concerns whether transfer in discrimination learning is based upon responding to absolute features of the stimuli or upon responding to patterns or relations among stimuli. We can best illustrate this controversy by examining a simple experiment.

Chickens were trained to respond to the darker of two grays by rewarding the animals with food when they responded to the darker and by not rewarding them when they responded to the lighter (Kohler, 1925). After this discrimination was reliably established, the animals were presented with a new discrimination task, in which they had to choose between the original reinforced gray and one which was still darker. In the new task, the animals responded to the darker of the two grays, even though they had always been rewarded for choosing the other gray. Kohler argued on the basis of these findings that the animals had learned to respond to the relationship between the stimuli—that is, the relationship of "darker than," rather than to the absolute properties of the stimuli. In contrast, if the animals were learning to respond to absolute properties of the stimuli, they should have responded to the gray which was originally rewarded.

This phenomenon of responding to a new discrimination task on the basis of relationships among stimuli is called *transposition*. For a long time, it was argued by Gestalt psychologists as evidence against stimulus-response conceptions of discrimination learning that presumably contended that organisms respond to the absolute properties of stimuli.

Spence (1937) has presented a theory of discrimination learning which accounts for transposition within the framework of stimulus-response theory. The advantage of his theory is that it provides a way of predicting transposition from established principles of behavior. Briefly, the theory views discrimination learning as based upon the gradual accrual of response strength. First, when a response to a particular stimulus is reinforced, a gradient of stimulus generalization about that stimulus develops. Second, when a response to another stimulus is nonreinforced, a gradient of generalized extinction about that stimulus will develop. In other words, there is less of a tendency to respond to stimuli that are similar to the nonreinforced stimulus. Third, the gradients of stimulus generalization and extinction summate algebraically so that the tendency to respond to any stimulus along the dimension tested is obtained by subtracting the gradient of extinction from the gradient of stimulus generalization. In short, we must subtract the weakened tendency to respond produced by generalized extinction from the positive tendency to respond produced by stimulus generalization.

Spence showed how this theory could apply to discrimination learning by first training chimpanzees to respond to a square which was 256 sq cm in size and not to respond to a square which was 160 sq cm in size. He then presented the animals with a new discrimination in which the stimuli were 256 sq cm and 409 sq cm and found that the animals responded to the larger stimulus. Spence explained this relational responding in terms of the algebraic summation theory described above. Accordingly, the gradient of extinction had sufficiently weakened the tendency to respond to the 256 stimulus so that the tendency to respond to the 409 stimulus was greater. A tendency to respond to the 409 stimulus developed because of stimulus generalization and, in turn, relatively little extinction generalized to the 409 stimulus.

Subsequent studies have been directed toward specifying the conditions under which transposition or its failure occurs. For example, Ehrenfreund (1952) and Kendler (1950) have shown that transposition depends on the degree of separation between the two stimuli. As the distance between the stimuli increases, the amount of relational responding is reduced, which is in accord with Spence's theory. Kuenne (1946) has shown that transposition is also a function of age, with younger children showing more evidence for breakdown in transposition.

Recently, some limitations in Spence's formulation have been noted. First, on logical grounds Bugelski (1956) has noted that it is impossible to predict what might happen in a transposition experiment according to Spence's theory because of possible differences in the shape of the generalization gradient. Bugelski notes that Spence's theory is based on the assumption that the gradients of generalization and extinction follow a concave pattern, whereas if such gradients were convex in shape, then different predictions would follow. In a slightly different vein, Riley (1958) has contended that Spence's assumption that animals do respond to the absolute properties of stimuli is itself unacceptable. Riley has proposed that the effective stimuli in a discrimination learning task must be regarded as involving a relationship between contrasting parts of a stimulus complex. As a test of this "contrast hypothesis," Riley reported that the usual breakdown in transposition with stimuli far apart was not obtained as long as a contrast between the test figure and background stimulation was maintained.

Rudel (1958) has reported a U-shaped transposition function with children; relational responses were obtained with near and far tests and no relational responses were obtained with tests in the midrange of the stimulus continuum. Finally, Wohlwill (1962) has shown that the tendency to make relational as distinct from absolute responses can depend on the way in which the stimuli are presented. Children were first presented with an array of two sets of stimuli, one group always being reinforced for choosing the smaller number of the two arrays, and the other group was always reinforced for making an absolute choice. During the test series, the stimuli were presented in several different ways and relational or absolute responses were made depending upon the manner in which they were presented. For example, if the stimuli were presented in the form of scattered arrays of dots (perceptual series), the subjects readily made a relational choice, whereas if the stimuli were presented not as an array of dots but as numerals (symbolic series), the absolute choice was made more frequently. These as well as other findings suggest that the classic Spence position, although extremely useful, will have to be modified or expanded in order to account for such results.

A Two-Stage Theory of Learning

A recent significant development in verbal learning has been the construction of a two-stage theory of paired-associate learning (for example, Hovland and Kurtz, 1952, Underwood, Runquist, and Schulz, 1959, Underwood and Schulz, 1960). Although this theory was initially developed to interpret certain features of paired-associate learning, it appears to be applicable to the analysis of transfer phenomena as well. This theory regards paired-associate learning as consisting of two fairly distinct stages: *response integration* and *associative "hook-up."* Accordingly, the first stage in learning a list of paired-associates is response integration; in this stage the subject learns to differentiate each response in the list from others. In other words, the response becomes highly available to the subject. After the response becomes integrated, the subject then learns to associate it with its approprite stimulus.

Although the two-stage theory has been applied largely to the learning of paired-associate lists, Ellis and Burnstein (1960) have advocated extending this theory to the learning of two successive paired-associate lists—that is, to the analysis of transfer of training. Accordingly, they analyzed the *A–B, C–B* paradigm in which the same responses are made to new stimuli in the transfer task. With this paradigm, positive transfer can occur as a result of response learning that takes place in the first list. If the responses are well integrated, then learning of the second list can begin with the second or "hook-up" stage. With this conception, they were able to interpret several findings which involve transfer as a function of the time elapsing between the original and transfer tasks. First, with paired-associate tasks containing highly meaningful responses such as adjectives, transfer was found to remain roughly constant with the passage of time (Ellis, 1958). This finding suggested that the constancy of the transfer-time function was largely dependent upon the operation of the associative or "hook-up" stage since the responses were already well integrated. Next, if the responses are low in meaningfulness, such as nonsense syllables, transfer declines with the passage of time (Ellis and Burnstein, 1960). Although the responses in the transfer task are the same as those in the training task, they are subject to some loss from forgetting, and thus must be partially relearned in the transfer task. Ellis and Burnstein thus reasoned that with the *A–B, C–B* paradigm, transfer would show a greater loss with time as the response integration or relearning stage became increasingly important in learning the transfer list. In two subsequent studies (Ellis and Hunter, 1960 and 1961) results were obtained which supported this analysis.

In a recent study, Jung (1963) has also extended the two-stage theory in an attempt to account for additional phenomena in transfer. He assumed that in the *A–B, C–B* paradigm transfer in the learning of the second list would result from response learning in the first list. He then predicted that such transfer should be greater with responses of low meaning since low meaning responses require more response learning than do those of high meaning. His findings indicated greater *relative* transfer following practice with low meaning responses. This was the case when the effects of nonspecific transfer were removed through the use of an *A–B, C–D* control group.

LEARNING SET THEORY

Although we have described the work of Harlow [3] [1] on the establishment of learning sets in an earlier chapter, a few additional points need mentioning. Learning set formation, as we noted, represents the transfer between many problems of a single class over a considerable time span as distinct from short-term studies of transfer based on only a few problems. In the course of acquisition of a learning set, the learning curve was observed to shift from a characteristic S-shaped curve to one in which the curve increased rapidly but was negatively accelerated.

These features of the learning curve make it possible to predict certain aspects of the efficiency of learning. If it is assumed that transfer is a function of the amount learned, then more trials should be given in the early problems in order to maximize transfer. Harlow (1959) suggested that one technique for maximizing the efficiency of learning was to run the animal, on any given problem, through those trials on which gain in learning is greatest. Once the animal reaches a point of diminishing returns in gain, then it is wasteful to continue the animal on this particular problem.

Learning set theory also leads to predictions about the effects of motivation on learning. During the early stages of learning a series of problems, learning is slower and the learner makes more errors. Errors may lead the learner to refuse to make more responses as well as to make more random behavior which is characteristic of responses to frustration. Harlow predicts that there would be fewer emotional responses as a learning set develops because of fewer errors being produced. Finally, he suggests that the resistance that some elderly people show to new learning situations may be associated more with frustration arising from making errors than with any limitations in learning capacity.

[1] Bracketed numbers refer to readings in Part Two.

Harlow (1959) has extended his work on learning sets to include a detailed analysis of the kinds of errors that individuals make in discrimination learning situations. This analysis has led to the development of *error factor theory* that has been used to explain a variety of learning set phenomena. He has identified four types of error factors present in the typical discrimination learning problem which are called stimulus perseveration, differential cue, response shift, and position habit errors. His view of learning is that it involves the progressive suppression of these various error factors, indeed, that learning may be nothing more than the suppression or inhibition of error factors. Although this is an interesting view, it remains to be seen if such a view can account for all learning.

MATHEMATICAL MODELS IN TRANSFER

The last few years have seen the rapid growth of mathematical models in psychology. Detailed accounts of these can be seen in several sources (for example, Atkinson, 1963, Bush and Estes, 1959, Estes, 1959). Mathematical models have a number of advantages, including increased conceptual rigor, increased ability to predict events in an unequivocal fashion, and increased likelihood of detecting unstated assumptions. In the long run, mathematical models have the virtue of simplifying theory by clearing away assumptions which may be unnecessary for accurate prediction of behavior.

Only a brief account of one mathematical model will be given. Bower (1961 and 1962) has constructed a mathematical model for predicting performance in a paired-associate learning task. More specifically, the model is designed to predict the probability of the subject making an error on a given trial. First, Bower's model assumes that the stimulus element—that is, the stimulus item in a stimulus-response pair—is in one of two states, either conditioned or unconditioned to the correct response. Second, he assumes that on each reinforced trial the probability of a transition from an unconditioned to a conditioned state is a constant c. The learning rate c represents the probability that a stimulus item that is unconditioned will become conditioned or associated to its appropriate response as the result of a single reinforced trial. Consequently, the probability that an item will remain unconditioned is $1 - c$. More generally, the probability that an item will remain unconditioned after n reinforced trials is $(1 - c)^n$.

The model also takes into account the number of response alternatives (N) that are available to the subject. Suppose there are only four responses in a paired-associate list. Then the subject has a chance of correctly guessing the response one out of four times. More generally, Bower states that if the stimulus element is in an unconditioned state, then the probability of a correct response due to guessing is $1/N$. In order for $1/N$ to represent validly the probability of a correct guess, the model assumes that all responses are equiprobable. With these assumptions, the probability of an incorrect guess is $1 - (1/N)$.

The probability that a subject will make an error on a given trial is designated as q_n. The value of q_n for a given trial is the probability that an item will fail to be conditioned multiplied by the probability that the subject will make an incorrect guess. The probability that a subject will make an error on a given trial is:

$$q_n = (1 - \frac{1}{N}) \ (1 - c)^{n-1} \qquad (1)$$

A virtue of Bower's model is its simplicity, namely, that it can predict the probability of an error on a given trial from just two events. He has shown that this model is quite applicable to paired-associate learning—that is, he has shown good agreement between the predicted and empirical results in paired-associate learning.

Rickert (1963) in an unpublished study, has advocated extending this model to the study of paired-associate transfer. He assumed that the learning process which underlies the "associative" stage in a transfer task is the same as that in the acquisition of a list of paired-associates. In addition, he assumed that if the stimulus items in the transfer task were similar to those in the original task, then a certain proportion of the items will already be conditioned on the first trial of the transfer task. These two assumptions imply that the effect of stimulus similarity on transfer is to shift the intercept constant of the learning curve, but that the rate will remain the same in the course of transfer. In other words, performance on the transfer task is shifted so that learners start at a higher initial level, compared with controls, but learn at the same rate. Rickert's findings indicate that the agreement between the predicted and empirical findings is quite high, thus supporting the usefulness of his proposal to extend Bower's model to paired-associate transfer.

IX

Some Final Comments

THE PREVIOUS CHAPTERS SHOULD LEAVE THE READER with a picture of transfer as an area that is actively engaging the attention of many researchers but is, at the same time, an area deficient in some respects. Perhaps the most striking impression one receives from an examination of the current status of transfer is that it is relatively strong in empirical findings and somewhat weaker in the development of theory. Until fairly recently, research in transfer has been rather heavily oriented toward the establishment of functional relationships between various classes of independent and dependent variables with only limited effort at integrating such relationships into some theoretical framework.

There appears to be at least two explanations for this lag in theoretical development. First, transfer has long been a source of concern to those involved with practical applied problems. Much of the early research in transfer was devoted to exploring the conditions which influenced or produced transfer in the classroom. Heavy emphasis was placed on questions which had direct, practical implications for the classroom teacher. Thus, it is not too surprising that developments in theory lagged behind those which were regarded as more pressing.

The second reason for this delay in the development of theory appears to be a function of the relative "complexity" of transfer as compared with some other areas of learning. When psychologists first began to construct behavior systems (for example, Hull, 1943, Tolman, 1932), emphasis was placed on relatively simple kinds of learning tasks for which a high degree of laboratory control was possible. Indeed, the trend has been toward using increasingly simple learning situations for the purposes of testing and developing behavior theory. Related to this second point was the hope, or assumption, that more complex or higher-order phenomena like transfer might be explained in terms of simpler or lower-level concepts. Thus, if a psychologist were especially concerned with theoretical problems as related to transfer, he would more likely attempt to formalize a conception of, say, stimulus generalization as distinct from the more inclusive concept of transfer.

In the last few years, however, there has been a distinct effort at strengthening and developing theoretical conceptions of transfer. Much of this effort has stemmed from work in paired-associate verbal learning, which has served as an extremely useful analytical device (for example, Underwood and Schulz, 1960). Similarly, the work in stimulus predifferentiation and related effort in transfer and perceptual learning (for example, Vanderplas, 1958 and 1963) are additional areas which are beginning to show theoretical development. Although predictions in science are always risky, three areas of transfer which appear to have much promise in the development of more systematic conceptions of transfer are those of paired-associate verbal learning, especially as related to the two-stage hypothesis, stimulus predifferentiation, and mediation.

Another need is greater standardization in research procedures and equipment that will increase the comparability of findings from different laboratories. We saw that in the case of transfer and task difficulty, it was extremely difficult to make any systematic generalizations about the role of task difficulty in transfer because many different kinds of tasks have been used. Similarly, we saw that divergencies, of both findings and theoretical interpretations, in studies of transfer of predifferentiation could be accounted for, in part, by differences in criterion measures of transfer. Much more careful attention to the parameters of the experiment itself, as well as to procedures and equipment, must be given if generalizations are to be readily obtained. One area where standardization has been achieved to a high degree is paired-associate learning, which may be one reason why this task appeals to many research workers.

Finally, more efforts toward a taxonomy of tasks would also aid progress, not only in transfer, but in the field of learning in general. Gagné (1962) has made some progress in this direction by developing a taxonomy of tasks based upon a hierarchy of learner capabilities. One of his major concerns is the proper sequencing of tasks —that is, the specification of various subtask learnings necessary for the learning of more complex tasks in the hierarchy. In addition, Gagné has proposed a research program in which one begins with extremely simple tasks, such as discrimination, and investigates transfer of training to tasks of progressively greater complexity. In a similar vein, a recent symposium (Melton, 1964) was devoted to the attempt of relating various gross categories of learning. One obvious advantage of a task taxonomy is that it permits one to relate his work to a more general conceptual scheme and, in addition, to provide ultimately a scheme for predicting transfer of training from one level to another.

PART TWO

The Selected Readings

[1] B. J. Underwood, "Associative Transfer in Verbal Learning as a Function of Response Similarity and Degree of First-List Learning"

[2] C. E. Osgood, "The Similarity Paradox in Human Learning: A Resolution"

[3] H. F. Harlow, "The Formation of Learning Sets"

[4] W. A. Russell and L. H. Storms, "Implicit Verbal Chaining in Paired-Associate Learning"

[5] C. P. Duncan, "Transfer After Training with Single Versus Multiple Tasks"

[6] H. C. Ellis and D. G. Muller, "Transfer in Perceptual Learning Following Stimulus Predifferentiation"

[7] B. B. Hudgins, "Effects of Group Experiences on Individual Problem Solving"

[1]

Associative Transfer in Verbal Learning as a Function of Response Similarity and Degree of First-List Learning

BENTON J. UNDERWOOD [1]

The importance of response similarity in associative transfer has been well established by several recent experiments in verbal learning (Haagen, 1943, Morgan and Underwood, 1950, Osgood, 1946). In the study most pertinent to the present investigation (Morgan and Underwood, 1950), it was shown that with identical stimuli in two paired-adjectives lists, positive transfer to the second list was related directly to response similarity. These findings were interpreted as being produced by response generalization. It was known from another study (Underwood and Hughes, 1950) that if errors made on a retention test of a single list were scaled for their similarity to the correct response (which the error replaced), frequency of errors and similarity were related directly—there was a gradient of generalized responses. Thus, in the theory of response generalization accounting for transfer phenomena, use was made also of a gradient of response generalization.[2]

The theory as applied to transfer phenomena will be summarized. It is assumed that when Response B is learned to Stimulus A, there will also exist a certain associative strength between A and items similar to B. Following the implication of the demonstrated gradient of generalized responses, it is assumed further that the strength of any given generalized response tendency is directly indexed by the similarity between the generalized response and Response B. In effect, when B is being attached to Stimulus A, many associations

---

[1] These experiments were made possible by a grant from The Graduate School, Northwestern University.

[2] This theory is similar to one proposed earlier by Osgood (1946).

SOURCE: B. J. Underwood, "Associative Transfer in Verbal Learning as a Function of Response Similarity and Degree of First-List Learning," *The Journal of Experimental Psychology*, 1951, 42, 44–54. Reprinted by permission of B. J. Underwood and the American Psychological Association.

between A and responses similar to B are also being built up. It is as if these similar responses are parasitically reinforced. These generalized associations do not, of course, gain associative strength as rapidly as does the connection which is reinforced directly $(A–B)$.

With the above conception of the operation of response generalization, transfer effects which resulted from variation in response similarity could be readily accounted for. If S learns $A–B$ (first list) and then learns $A–B$ (second list with identical stimuli and highly similar responses), high positive transfer should result in learning $A–B_1$. This should occur because Stimulus A, as a consequence of first-list learning, has acquired a suprathreshold tendency to elicit B_1 even before the second list is presented. When $A–B_1$ is directly reinforced in learning the second list, its response strength *appears* to build up very rapidly. As the theory interprets this rapid acquisition, however, it is because $A–B_1$ was already an established connection. As the second-list responses decrease in similarity to Response B, the less should be the positive transfer.

A further implication of the theory is that in learning the second list under the above conditions, intrusions from the first list to the second will be greatest with highest response similarity. When the strength of connection $A–B_1$ becomes about equal to that of $A–B$, discrimination between response tendencies should be low. This was the finding in the previous study; with highly similar responses between the two lists a great many intrusions occurred in second-list learning. Yet, even with this great response competition, positive transfer was high.

If the above conception of response generalization is to be maximally useful as an explanatory device for transfer effects, the influence of other manipulable variables (in addition to similarity) must be incorporated. The major purpose of the present investigation was to test the theory as it is expanded to include degree of first-list learning. The expansion consists simply of a formal statement that as degree of learning of $A–B$ (first list) increases, the strength of generalized responses increases. This assumption implies that as response similarity is held constant, amount of positive transfer will increase as degree of first-list learning increases. Data from the previous study were analyzed with this expectation in mind, and some support was found for the prediction. However, the range of first-list response strengths available was too restricted to establish the generality of the finding. Therefore, the present experiments were designed to explore thoroughly the relationships among degree of first-list learning, response similarity, and positive transfer.

The postulated relationships between degree of first-list learning and response similarity are diagrammed in Figure 1. This figure

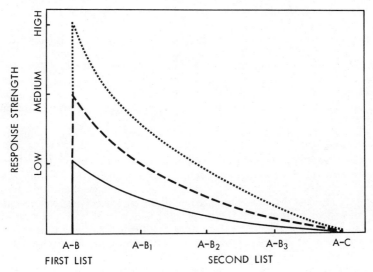

FIGURE 1. Theoretical gradients of generalized responses as related to degree of first-list learning and similarity between responses in the first and second lists.

pictures three degrees of first-list learning, the first list being again symbolized by *A–B*. As *A–B* is increased in strength by direct reinforcement, it is assumed that the gradient of response-generalization also rises. This means that generalized response tendencies ($A–B_1$, $A–B_2$, $A–B_3$) are also increased in strength. Highly similar responses ($A–B_1$) gain more in strength as first-list learning increases than do those of low similarity ($A–B_3$). If the response is not similar to *B* (Response *C*), no increase in response strength will occur as first-list learning increases.

From Figure 1 an unambiguous prediction can be made concerning positive transfer in learning the second list when both similarity and degree of first-list learning are varied; specifically, the greater the response similarity and the higher the degree of first-list learning, the greater the positive transfer.

PROCEDURE

MATERIALS.   The lists of 12 paired adjectives used in the experiment were constructed by Haagen (1943). Illustrations of the different degrees of sealed synonymity used to vary response similarity are available elsewhere (Morgan and Underwood, 1950). For the present experiments only three degrees of response synonymity have been used, to be designated here as high, medium, and low, the latter being zero degree of scaled similarity—comparable to Response C in Figure 1.[3] Each of the three degrees of similarity is represented by two lists of 12 pairs of words. Both lists have identical stimuli with the synonymity obtaining between the responses of these identical stimuli. In two previous experiments (Haagen, 1943, Morgan and Underwood, 1950) it was shown that the sets of lists did not 'differ significantly in difficulty. A Hull-type drum was used to present the lists at the standard 2-sec. rate.

CONDITIONS.   For each of the three degrees of response similarity used, three degrees of first-list learning have been employed, for a total of nine conditions. These nine conditions have been executed in three experiments of three conditions each. In Experiment I the first list was presented until S gave four correct responses on a single trial; in Experiment II the first list was presented until seven correct responses were given, and in Experiment III, the first list was learned to a criterion of two successive errorless trials. Degree of first-list learning was thus varied from experiment to experiment. The three conditions within each experiment differed only in terms of response similarity.

On all nine conditions the second list was learned until S anticipated seven responses on a single trial. Following the learning of the second list, S rested 20 min., then recalled and relearned the second list to one perfect trial.[4]

Differences in degree of learning and similarity among the conditions are summarized in Table 1. The three degrees of response synonymity will hereafter be referred to as H (high), M (medium), and L (low). Therefore, if a reference is given to II (L) it would mean Experiment II (in which degree of first-list learning was seven correct responses), Condition L (low response synonymity).

Order of the three conditions of similarity was counterbalanced in each experiment. With three conditions, a block of six Ss will effect complete balancing. Three such blocks were used in each experiment; hence, the

[3] These three degrees of similarity were Conditions B, D, and F in the previously reported study (Morgan and Underwood, 1950).

[4] Recalling the second list after the rest interval completes the proactive inhibition paradigm. However, the data on proactive inhibition will not be presented. The results on *learning* the second list will show that the acceleration of these second-list learning curves varied markedly for the various conditions. This, in effect, makes degree of second-list learning different for the conditions and vitiates meaningful comparisons for recall and relearning. This problem has been discussed in detail elsewhere (Underwood, 1949a, p. 529).

TABLE 1

Conditions Used to Determine Influence of
Response Similarity and Degree of List 1
Learning on Associative Transfer

Exp.	Cond.	Response Similarity	Degree of List-1 Learning
I	H	High	
I	M	Medium	4 correct
I	L	Low	responses
II	H	High	
II	M	Medium	7 correct
II	L	Low	responses
III	H	High	
III	M	Medium	2 successive
III	L	Low	errorless trials

number of Ss in each experiment was 18, or a total of 54 in all three
experiments. Each condition of similarity is represented by two lists.
Each of these lists appeared half the time as List 1, and half the time as
List 2. Therefore, any difference in difficulty of the two lists within a set
will not confound the transfer effects due to response similarity.

One practice day was given before the three experimental sessions.
All Ss learned the same lists on this day, the responses in the two lists
having medium similarity. Conditions on the practice day were identical
to those on the experimental days with regard to degree of learning. On
all conditions the interval between learning List 1 and List 2 was 30 sec.

RESULTS

Equality of Groups

The comparability of the learning of the three groups of Ss can
be demonstrated by comparing the mean number of trials to attain
four correct responses on the first list for all three experimental
conditions combined. Conditions for all three groups were identical
up to this point in learning the first list. The mean number of
trials required to reach the criterion of four correct responses was
$4.35\pm.39$, $4.37\pm.37$, and $4.09\pm.30$, for Experiments I, II, and III,
respectively. The largest difference is between Groups II and III,
but this difference, $.28\pm.48$, gives a t of only .58. Evaluation of

TABLE 2

**Mean Trials Required to Reach the Criteria of Learning
of the First List for All Conditions**

Cond.	Exp. I		Exp. II		Exp. III	
	Mean	*σM*	*Mean*	*σM*	*Mean*	*σM*
L	4.94	0.64	8.39	0.72	16.83	1.78
M	4.50	0.37	8.94	0.84	19.00	1.64
H	3.61	0.42	7.11	0.83	15.78	1.37

performance on the practice day also demonstrated the equality of the groups. It may be concluded that the groups are sufficiently comparable to allow direct interexperimental comparisons.

LIST-1 LEARNING. The mean number of trials required to attain the criteria of learning for the different experiments is shown in Table 2. Reference to these values will be made later when transfer effects in learning List 2 are noted.

Transfer Effects

TRIALS TO LEARN LIST 2. The mean number of trials required to reach the criterion of seven correct responses on the second list is the first index of transfer considered. The essential data are shown in Table 3, and graphed in Figure 2.[5] For purposes of plotting, the

TABLE 3

**Transfer Effects as Measured by Mean Trials to the Criterion
of Seven Responses on a Single Trial on List 2**

Cond.	Exp. I		Exp. II		Exp. III	
	Mean	*σM*	*Mean*	*σM*	*Mean*	*σM*
L	6.78	0.48	6.94	0.61	6.33	0.80
M	6.28	0.45	6.56	0.68	4.72	0.41
H	5.50	0.65	4.56	0.50	3.17	0.41

[5] Although Haagen (1943) and Morgan and Underwood (1950) found no appreciable differences in rate of learning the three sets of lists (unbiased by transfer), it will be noted throughout that the high-similarity lists tend to be learned more rapidly than the other two sets. Estimates of positive transfer will, therefore, be slightly overestimated for these lists.

three degrees of first-list learning will be considered as 4, 8, and 17 trials, for Experiments I, II, and III, respectively. As can be seen in Table 2, these values approximate the mean number of trials required to attain the criteria of first-list learning.

The transfer effects are clear-cut. With low response similarity there is little evidence for differential transfer as degree of first-list learning increases. As response similarity increases, the effect on learning the second list becomes marked, so that with high similarity and high degree of learning, positive transfer is at a maximum. The interaction between the two variables is evident in Figure 2. The magnitude of the absolute transfer effect with high similarity is large. On the average only 3.17 trials were required to learn the second list on Condition III (H), and this value includes the first or study trial on which S makes no anticipations. Of the 18 Ss, 8 gave seven or more correct responses on the second trial—the first anticipation trial.[6]

All transfer effects in Table 3 and Figure 2 are positive. This was determined by taking the mean number of trials required to attain the criterion of seven correct responses on the first list of Experiments II and III (Experiment I could not be included since learning was carried only to four correct responses). These positive transfer effects cannot, of course, be attributed entirely to the independent variable, since learning-how-to-learn transfer is also included. Negative transfer was present on the first anticipation trial of the second list when response similarity was low. Extensive data under comparable conditions have been presented elsewhere (Underwood, 1949b), so are not repeated.

A MORE DIRECT TEST OF THE RESPONSE-GENERALIZATION HYPOTHESIS. The data presented above give support to the hypothesis advanced in the introduction to this paper. But a more direct test of the generalization hypothesis may be obtained by making an analysis of the strength of each item in List 1 and then determining what happens to the corresponding item in List 2 on the *first anticipation*

---

[6] Evidence on reliability of the differences are given in the following *t*-values. For I (L) vs. III (L), *t* is .48; I (M) vs. III (M), *t* is 2.56; I (H) vs. III (H), *t* is 3.03. Since these intercondition comparisons are based on uncorrelated data, there are 34 *df*. A *t* of 2.72 is significant at the .01 level of confidence, and a *t* of 2.03 is significant at the .05 level. Intracondition comparisons for the extremes of the similarity dimension are as follows: I (L) vs. I (H), *t* is 2.51; II (L) vs. II (H), *t* is 3.72. With these correlated data there are 17 *df*. A *t* of 2.11 is significant at the .05 level, and a *t* of 2.89 is required for the .01 level.

trial of List 2. From this analysis it is possible to derive gradients of response evocation which allow direct inference concerning the role of generalized responses with varying degrees of learning. The method of analysis is somewhat complex and is, therefore, reported in detail.

Degree of learning of List 1 is "varied" in the analysis by determining the number of correct responses (reinforcements) for each item. Items having the same number of reinforcements may then be

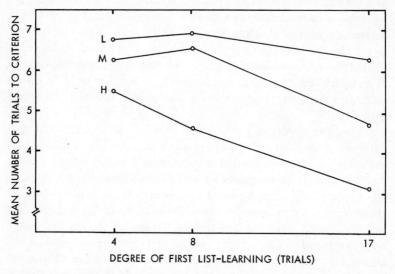

FIGURE 2. Transfer as a function of response similarity and degree of first-list learning. *L* refers to low response similarity, *M* to medium, and *H* to high similarity.

pooled. Such a procedure eliminates the need for keeping the three experiments distinct. Each list had 12 items. Since 18 Ss served in each of the nine conditions, the total number of items available is $12 \times 18 \times 9$, or 1,944 items. In order that the values will be stable, response strengths on List 1 have been combined in such a fashion that none of the categories has less than one hundred cases. With three degrees of synonymity and four levels of response strength, there are 12 categories. Thus, each item of the first list has a known degree of learning and a known degree of similarity to the corresponding item in List 2. According to the hypothesis, if generalization is operating to build up the response strength of similar responses while responses in List 1 are being learned, the probability of obtaining a correct response on the first trial of List 2 should be related directly to degree of similarity and degree of learning of responses in List 1.

The data are shown in Table 4. "Number of Cases" indicates the number of items in a given classification of similarity and response strength. For example, with high similarity, there were 182 items which received one or two reinforcements during the learning of List 1. On the first anticipation trial of List 2, 61 of the corresponding items were correctly anticipated. Or, of the 182 items, 33.5 per cent were correct on the first trial.

TABLE 4

Transfer as a Function of Response Similarity and Degree
of Learning as Determined by Item Analysis of List 1
and the First Anticipation Trial of List 2

Similarity	Measure	Number of Reinforcements			
		0	1–2	3–6	7 and over
Low	No. Cases	167	173	126	182
	No. Correct	13	14	17	20
	% Correct	7.8	8.1	13.5	11.0
Medium	No. Cases	183	148	104	213
	No. Correct	13	20	31	57
	% Correct	7.1	13.5	29.8	26.8
High	No. Cases	180	182	123	163
	No. Correct	25	61	61	73
	% Correct	13.9	33.5	49.6	44.8

In general, the data in this table confirm the transfer effects measured by trials to learn the second list. However, an additional fact is shown which was apparently obscured by the analysis made in terms of gross trials. This fact is that when a List 1 item has been reinforced seven or more times, the per cent correct on the first trial of List 2 is consistently less than when the number of reinforcements is in the range of from three to six. The amount of reduction is not great but is present with all degrees of similarity.

Further examination of the table shows clearly how response generalization appears to provide parasitic reinforcement. When items in List 2 have high response similarity to those of List 1, and when the first-list items have been reinforced from three to six times, nearly 50 per cent responses are given correctly on the first anticipation trial. As similarity and degree of learning decrease, the percentage of correct responses on the first trial of List 2 decreases.

The question may be raised as to how generalized or parasitic reinforcement compares in magnitude with direct reinforcement. An approximate answer can be given. All List 1 learning for Experiments II and III was analyzed to determine the number of correct responses given each item up to but not including the trial on which S gave seven correct anticipations. Whether or not the item was given correctly on the criterial trial was also recorded. The per cent correct on this criterial trial for each of four levels of reinforcement was then determined. For zero reinforcements the per cent correct was 33.1; for 1 to 2 reinforcements, 72.0; for 3 to 6 reinforcements, 91.6, and for 7 or more reinforcements, the per cent correct was 97.4. Thus, these values give the probability of an item's being correct on the immediately succeeding trial as a function of number of times it has been *directly reinforced* before that trial.

These values on the influence of direct reinforcement may be plotted as having maximum similarity along a dimension of response similarity. That is, since these percentages were derived from continuous-learning data, they may be thought of as representing identity of responses and stimuli. The response-generalization data in Table 4 may then be ranged on the same continuum of similarity. The high-similarity condition is just one step removed from identity, since it consists of identical stimuli and highly similar responses. Putting the two sets of data on the same graph will provide a visual comparison of the effect of direct reinforcement as compared with the response strength built up by generalization of responses. The curves are shown in Figure 3.[7]

[7] It was indicated previously that the comparative influence of direct reinforcement and reinforcement through generalization would be rough. The reasons for this are apparent now that the method of analysis has been described. The influence of the study trial (Trial 1) of List 2 on the responses given on Trial 2 cannot be determined. But it seems obvious that the magnitude of parasitic reinforcement, as inferred from responses on Trial 2, would be somewhat

These curves may be taken as rough estimates of gradients of generalized responses as a function of degree of learning of the directly reinforced items. Clearly, the gradients are elevated as degree of learning is increased, with the elevation being greater the greater the response similarity. As noted previously, a reversal in the general relationship occurs with high response strength. This

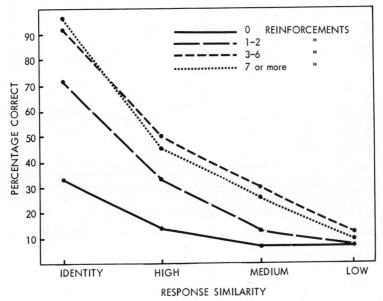

FIGURE 3. Relative influence of generalized reinforcement and direct reinforcement.

reversal may be interpreted to mean that with high degrees of learning of the first-list response, some differentiation (reduction in generalization) is established without apparent differential reinforcement. Gibson (1940, p. 206) has suggested that this may occur in the case of stimulus generalization. Thus, as a consequence of sheer repetition of the correct association, some differentiation of this response from other similar responses is established.[8]

overestimated because of the effect of the study trial. On the other hand, the short interval between learning List 1 and learning List 2 might, because of forgetting, tend to underestimate the effects of parasitic reinforcement as compared with direct reinforcement.

[8] In experiments in which similarity is manipulated, there is the possibility that the transfer effects are in part a function of S's giving responses which he

OVERT INTRUSIONS DURING LIST 2 LEARNING. In the previous paper it was found that as response similarity increased, number of intrusions during learning of the second list also increased. The intrusion data from List 2 learning for the present experiments are plotted in Figure 4. To obtain the values, the total number of intru-

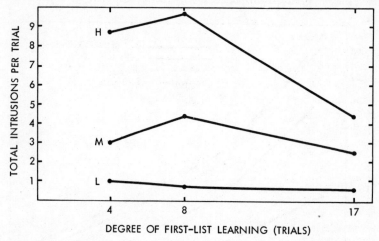

FIGURE 4. Frequency of intrusions as a function or response similarity and degree of first-list learning. *L* refers to low response similarity, *M* to medium, and *H* to high similarity.

sions for all 18 Ss was divided by number of trials required to reach the criterion of seven responses on List 2. This division is necessary to equalize for trial differences.

With low similarity very few intrusions occur, and no observable difference is evident as a function of degree of List 1 learning. With medium similarity of responses, frequency of intrusions first increases and then decreases as a function of degree of List 1 learning. The greatest number of intrusions occurs with high similarity of responses, with maximum frequency obtaining for moderate degrees

---

thinks might fit the similarity of a given condition. Thus, if the first-list response was *dirty*, S might think to himself that *filthy* or *unclean* are likely second-list responses. He might give one of these responses to the appropriate stimulus word, and one could not readily account for this response on the basis of generalization as it is outlined in this paper. However, the fact that the gradient reverses with high degrees of learning—a condition which should be favorable for S to "prepare" responses for the second list—suggests that this problem is not a serious one.

of List 1 learning—Condition II (H). These data from Experiment II are exactly the same as found under comparable conditions in the previous experiment. The additional fact provided by the present experiments is that with high degrees of List 1 learning, intrusions decrease so that no simple relationship between similarity and frequency of intrusions exists. Rather, similarity and degree of learning interact to produce the intrusions. To compete, incompatible response tendencies must be nearly equal. With the high degrees of learning used here for List 1 of Experiment III, few List 2 items would reach the level of the response strength of their corresponding List 1 items. Thus, the reduction in frequency of intrusions with high degrees of learning is to be accounted for by the fact that potentially competing responses failed to attain equal response strengths. Had the learning of the second list been carried to a higher criterion, many more intrusions should have been observed.

DISCUSSION

The major findings of the present experiment are: (1) as degree of response similarity and first-list learning increases, associative facilitation, as measured by trials to learn the second list, increases; (2) frequency of intrusions from the first list occurring during the learning of the second list increases as response similarity increases, and initially increases and then decreases as degree of first-list learning increases.

The item analysis has allowed construction of empirical curves (Figure 3) which closely approximate those to be expected on the basis of a response generalization theory as outlined in the introduction. An exception to the theory discovered in the analysis is that with very high degrees of first-item learning, positive transfer early in the learning of the corresponding second-list item is somewhat less than if the degree of learning were lower. This has been interpreted as indicating that some differentiation or restriction in generalization is accomplished by mere repetition of a connection. How such differentiation could take place is not suggested by the data.

The present data, and those obtained previously (Morgan and Underwood, 1950), demonstrate that it is possible to have high positive transfer and high interference (as indexed by intrusions) produced by the same conditions. The interference takes place when two response tendencies are about equal in strength. The high positive transfer through generalization takes place when the directly reinforced response is stronger than the generalized response. It is to be noted again, in support of this analysis, that when the first list was learned to a high degree, fewer intrusions occurred in learning the second list than when the first list was taken to a more moderate level of learning. These facts suggest further that unlearning or weakening of a first-list response through nonreinforcement of it in learning the second list, may not take place unless the second-list ifitem becomes as strong as the first-list item.

Finally, the data presented show that response similarity is an extremely important factor in transfer in verbal learning. In fact, on a theoretical basis, response similarity appears to produce greater variation in transfer effects than does comparable variation in stimulus similarity (Underwood, 1949a, p. 303). On the basis of the data available, response generalization appears to be a useful theoretical tool to account for the empirical facts produced by manipulation of response similarity, just as stimulus generalization is useful in accounting for the influence of variation in stimulus similarity.

SUMMARY

The present experiments tested the hypothesis that associative facilitation in paired-associates learning is directly related to interlist response similarity and degree of first-list learning. The prediction follows from a theory of response generalization. Three experiments were performed in each of which there were three degrees of response synonymity. In the two lists of 12 paired adjectives used for a given condition of similarity, the stimuli were identical. The three experiments differed only in degree of first-list learning, which was four correct responses on a single trial, seven correct on a single trial, or two successive perfect trials. The criterion of learning for the second list was always seven correct responses on a single trial. The conditions were counterbalanced among the 18 Ss serving in each experiment.

The major results were:

1. As measured by mean number of trials required to reach the criterion of seven correct responses on a single trial of the second list, positive transfer was related directly to response similarity and degree of first-list learning.

2. An item analysis showed the relationship among degree of first-item learning, similarity, and the probability of correctly anticipating the second-list item on the first trial. This analysis allowed construction of response-evocation gradients which closely approximated those expected on the basis of a theory of response generalization. These gradients confirmed the transfer effects mentioned above with the exception that with very high degrees of learning, the relationship breaks down.

3. Frequency of intrusions from the first list which occurred during the learning of the second were related directly to similarity. However, as degree of first-list learning increased, frequency of intrusions first increased and then decreased.

[2]
The Similarity Paradox in Human Learning: A Resolution

CHARLES E. OSGOOD

Behavior is a continuous, fluid process, and activities learned in the laboratory are as much a part of it as a trip to the county fair. The segments which an experimenter arbitrarily selects for analysis are inextricably imbedded in this expanding matrix and are interpretable only in terms of its interactions. Transfer and retroaction experiments are explicit attempts to gauge these interactions, and the similarity variable—that is, the homogeneities existing among the materials successively practiced—turns out to be the most important factor as well as the most puzzling.

The classic statement of the relation between similarity and interference in human learning, as found in most textbooks in psychology, is that "the greater the similarity, the greater the interference."

SOURCE: C. E. Osgood, "The Similarity Paradox in Human Learning: A Resolution," *The Psychological Review*, 1949, 56, 132–143. Reprinted by permission of C. E. Osgood and the American Psychological Association.

Although this law is traceable mainly to the work of McGeoch and his associates (Johnson, 1933, McGeoch and McDonald, 1931, McGeoch and McGeoch, 1937), there are many other experiments which superficially appear to substantiate it. When carried to its logical conclusions, however, this law leads to an impossible state of affairs. The highest degree of similarity of both stimulus and response in the materials successively practiced is that where any simple habit or S–R association is learned. The stimulus situation can never be precisely identical from trial to trial, nor can the response, but they are maximally similar—and here the greatest facilitation (ordinary learning) is obtained. *Ordinary learning, then, is at once the theoretical condition for maximal interference but obviously the practical condition for maximal facilitation.* Here is the fundamental paradox, and this paper suggests a resolution.

Empirical Laws of Transfer and Retroaction as Functions of Similarity

Transfer and retroaction in human learning are among the most extensively cultivated fields in experimental psychology, yet there are no clear-cut generalizations which satisfactorily bind the data together. The difficulty may be traced in part to the bewildering variety of procedures, materials and experimental designs employed by different investigators, a phenomenon perhaps characteristic of a young science. But some of the confusion can also be laid to the fact that in a large proportion of experiments the theoretically relevant relations are patently unspecifiable: the subjects merely learn List A and then List B, or Maze I and then Maze II, and either positive or negative effects may result, depending upon quite unanalyzable conditions. The purpose of this paper is to clarify the similarity function in human learning, and to accomplish this end only those experiments can be utilized wherein the *locus* of similarities is specifiable, as being between stimulus members, response members, or both. This analytic approach, although it may be considered inappropriate by some theorists and makes use of only part of the data, does give rise to a coherent and consistent picture.

When *transfer* is studied, one is interested in the effect of a specifiable prior activity upon the learning of a given test activity. When *retroaction* is studied, one is interested in the effect of a specifiable interpolated activity upon the retention of a previously learned activity. In both cases the experimenter arbitrarily "lifts" segments of a continuing process for analysis, and it would be expected that common laws would apply to both samplings. In the present context it can be shown that identical functions of similarity apply to both transfer and retroaction data, which simplifies the theoretical task considerably. Figure 1 gives symbolic representation to three basic learning paradigms, *A* that in which stimulus members are varied in the materials successively practiced while responses are functionally identical, *B* that in which responses are varied and stimuli are functionally identical, and *C* that in which both stimulus and response members are simultaneously varied. It will be seen that in so

Transfer and Retroaction Paradigms

TRANSFER

Paradigm A	$S_1 \rightarrow R_1$	$\underline{S_2} \rightarrow R_1$	$S_1 \rightarrow R_1$
Paradigm B	$S_1 \rightarrow R_1$	$S_1 \rightarrow \underline{R_2}$	$S_1 \rightarrow R_1$
Paradigm C	$S_1 \rightarrow R_1$	$\underline{S_2} \rightarrow \underline{R_2}$	$S_1 \rightarrow R_1$

RETROACTION

Figure 1. Paradigms indicating the locus of variation among the successively practiced materials. *A*, stimulus variation; *B*, response variation; *C*, simultaneous stimulus and response variation.

far as similarity relations are concerned, the test for transfer is simultaneously the interpolated activity when the entire retroactive sequence is followed. The term "functional identity" is used here to make explicit the fact that *true* identity among either stimulus or response processes is a will-o-the-wisp, approached but never attained. Functional identity of stimuli in successive trials or tasks exists when the situation is objectively constant (*i.e.*, when the same stimulus nonsense syllable appears on the screen or the same choice point is approached on repeated trials in the maze); functionally identical responses are those which the experimenter, at any given level of analysis, scores as being the same (*i.e.*, no matter how the subject says CYF or how the rat maneuvers about a turn, it is scored "correct"). Functional identity thus becomes the limiting case of maximum similarity.

1. Let us first consider *paradigm A*, the condition in which stim-

ulus similarity is variable and responses are functionally identical. The transfer portion of this paradigm will be recognized as nothing other than a symbolic statement of *stimulus generalization.* In Hovland's classic study (1937), for example, a galvanic skin response is first conditioned to a tone of a certain frequency (S_1–R_1), then the test tone is presented and the extent to which the same response is made to it measured (S_2–R_1). Hovland found that the greater the similarity between practice and test stimuli, the greater the amount of generalization (or positive transfer). The same results are regularly found wherever this paradigm can be identified, whether the materials be motor or verbal, meaningful or nonsense, or of any other nature. McKinney (1933) required subjects to respond with a correct letter upon seeing each of four geometrical designs and then measured transfer of the same responses to alterations of these designs; when Yum (1931) varied the similarity of visually presented nonsense-syllable stimuli, positive transfer was the result, the magnitude increasing with stimulus similarity.

While retroaction data derived from this paradigm are not so extensive, the available evidence is consistent in revealing *facilitation.* Hamilton's (1943) subjects learned lists of paired-associates in which the stimuli were geometrical forms and the responses were nonsense syllables. Although responses were "identical" on original and interpolated lists, the stimulus forms varied from "identity" through two degrees of similarity, as independently indexed in terms of generalization, to complete neutrality. The magnitude of retroactive facilitation decreased regularly as similarity among the stimulus members decreased, effects of approximately zero magnitude being obtained with neutral stimuli. The empirical law for this paradigm is: *where stimuli are varied and responses are functionally identical, positive transfer and retroactive facilitation are obtained, the magnitude of both increasing as the similarity among the stimulus members increases.*

2. The situation in which stimuli are constant and responses are varied, *paradigm B,* is the standard associative and reproductive inhibition paradigm and, as might be expected, a large number of experiments (*cf.* Bruce, 1933, Gibson, 1941, Underwood, 1945) testify to the fact that *interference* is produced under these conditions. However, there is also a large body of evidence showing positive transfer under the same conditions. The latter evidence may be

discounted on two grounds: (a) In many cases the so-called transfer response has been *learned previous* to the experimental situation. In many of Tolman's sign-learning studies, for example, animals trained to traverse the route to a goal by one path or means, such as running, will shift readily to another means, such as swimming, if the original behavior is blocked. Similarly, Wickens (1938) has shown that a human subject who has learned to avoid the shock which follows a tone by an extensor movement of his finger, when his palm is down, 'transfers' immediately to a flexion movement when his hand is then placed palm up. In such cases, the new learning in the experimental situation is the sign-value or meaning of the distinctive cue. A variety of overt behaviors has previously been associated with this mediation process—the human subject brings to the experiment a rich repertoire of pain-avoiding movements, and he would lift his head without new training if his nose were inserted between the electrodes! (b) In other cases what is measured as positive transfer under conditions fitting this paradigm can be shown to be attributable to *"practice effects,"* i.e., the subject is learning how to learn nonsense syllables or learning how to learn mazes, and these general skills or habits counteract the interference inherent in the design. Siipola (1941), for example, obtained small amounts of positive transfer for a code-substitution task, yet concluded from the large numbers of intrusions that actual negative transfer was being masked by a general "practice effect."

Bugelski (1942) required his subjects to learn an original list of 10 paired nonsense syllables (such as *toc-nem*) and then interpolated three additional lists, the experimental subjects having identical stimuli and varied responses (such as *toc-rul*) and the control subjects having both members varied (such as *cos-rul*). Although insignificant amounts of positive transfer to successive lists were obtained in both conditions, the inherent interfering character of the stimuli-identical paradigm was revealed in the fact that the experimental subjects showed a marked decrement upon relearning the first list while the controls showed continued facilitation. Clearest evidence for negative transfer and retroactive interference under the conditions of this paradigm is offered in a recent monograph by Underwood (1945). In measuring transfer, subjects learned 0, 2, 4, or 6 lists of meaningful paired-associates *prior* to learning a test list; in measuring retroaction, 0, 2, 4 or 6 interpolated lists were learned *after* the original learning of the same test list; in both cases, recall of the test list was measured after a delay of 25 minutes. Both negative transfer and retroactive interference were found, increasing in magnitude with the number of prior or interpolated lists having the same stimulus members but different responses.

But what about the *degree* of similarity among the varied responses in this paradigm? Perhaps because of the difficulty in defining response similarity, there are relatively few data here. In a recent experiment by Osgood (1946), original learning of a set of paired letter-pairs and meaningful adjectives (such as *c.m.–elated*) was followed by three types of interpolated items, each subject serving as his own control by learning an equal number of items in each similarity relation (such as *c.m.–high, c.m.–left,* or *c.m.–low*); all subjects finally relearned the original list. Although interference was obtained under all conditions, it was significantly *less* for similar meaningful relations. One of the conditions of Bruce's (1933) extensive investigation with nonsense-syllable paired-associates substantiates this finding. We may now state the empirical law for this paradigm: *where stimuli are functionally identical and responses are varied, negative transfer and retroactive interference are obtained, the magnitude of both decreasing as similarity between the responses increases.*

3. *Paradigm C,* where both stimuli and responses are simultaneously varied, is directly generated when the standard memory drum is used and lists of material are learned in constant serial order. Similarities are between items having the same serial position on successive lists, and each item serves simultaneously as a response to the preceding item and a stimulus for the succeeding item. Whatever interpolated lists are given, stimulus and response similarities must be simultaneously varied through the same degrees. McGeoch and McDonald, 1931 and Johnson, 1933 have employed this procedure with meaningful materials, finding retroactive interference to increase with the degree of similarity. Melton and Von Lackum, 1941 report the same result for nonsense syllables. McGeoch and McGeoch, 1937 and Johnson (1933) find the same result to hold for transfer when this paradigm is used.

An important experiment by Gibson (1941) also fits this paradigm. Her materials and procedures were identical with those reported above for Hamilton (1943). The Gibson experiment was actually the first of the series. Visual stimulus forms were varied through independently measured degrees of generalization, as was the case in Hamilton's study, but here responses were different and neutral. Negative transfer and retroactive interference were obtained, their magnitudes decreasing as stimulus similarity decreased and approximating zero with neutral stimuli. It should be noted that in both studies approximately zero transfer or retroaction was found when stimuli were neutral, regardless of response identity or difference. The empirical law for this paradigm: *when both stimulus and response members are simultaneously varied, negative transfer and retroactive interference are obtained, the magnitude of both increasing as the stimulus similarity increases.*

There are a considerable number of substantiating studies which have not been cited here, but if this writer's survey of the literature has been adequate, *there are no exceptions to the above empirical laws.* There are few studies where more than one relation is systematically explored, with the same materials, procedures and subjects, and for this reason it is difficult to quantify these relations. An exception is a study by Bruce (1933). One set of nonsense pairs (such as *req-kiv*) was learned by all subjects and transfer to several variations was measured: where stimuli were varied and responses were constant (*zaf-kiv* or *reb-kiv*) positive transfer was found as compared with a control condition, the amount being greater when stimuli were more similar: where responses were varied and stimuli were constant (*req vor*), negative transfer was found. The condition in which stimuli were constant and responses were highly similar (*req-kib*) was slightly superior to the control condition (both members neutral). Although this result appears to contradict the empirical law for this paradigm, it will be found to fit the hypothesis presented in the latter part of this paper: if ordinary learning is to be theoretically feasible, high degrees of response similarity must yield facilitation.

ATTEMPTED INTEGRATIONS OF THE DATA

A series of attempts to integrate the facts of transfer and retroaction can be traced in the history of this problem. As early as 1919 Wylie (1919) had made a distinction between stimulus and response activities, stating that the transfer effect is positive when an "old" response is associated with a new stimulus but negative when an "old" stimulus must be associated with a new response. "Old" in this context merely means that the member in question has previously been associated with another stimulus or response. This principle is valid, of course, within the limits of its gross differentiation. But (a) it takes account of neither stimulus nor response similarities and (b) it leaves the fundamental paradox untouched. Since successive responses are never precisely identical, even in ordinary learning, we are always associating stimuli with "new" responses and hence should inevitably get negative transfer.

Robinson was one of the first to perceive clearly this paradox and in 1927 he offered what is now known as the Skaggs-Robinson Hypothesis as a resolution. As shown in Figure 2, this hypothesis

THE SKAGGS-ROBINSON HYPOTHESIS

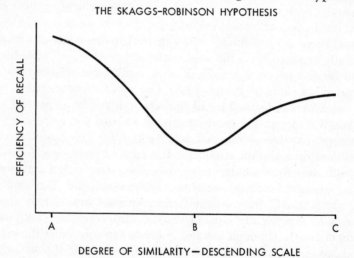

FIGURE 2. The Skaggs-Robinson Hypothesis: point *A* specifies maximum similarity (identity) and point *C* minimum similarity (neutrality) among the successively practiced materials; point *B* merely indicates the low point in the curve for efficiency of recall.

states that facilitation is greatest when successively practiced materials are identical (point *A*); facilitation is least, and hence interference maximal, with some moderate degree of similarity (point *B*); and facilitation increases again as we move toward neutrality (point *C*) but never attains the original level. Note that while point *A* defines maximum similarity (identity) and point *C* defines minimum similarity (neutrality), point *B* actually specifies no degree of similarity at all, but merely says that somewhere there is a low point in the facilitation curve. Several experiments (Cheng, 1929, Dreis, 1933, Harden, 1929, Kennelly, 1941, Robinson, 1927) combine to give rough validation to this poorly defined hypothesis, especially the A–B sector of it.

The series of studies by McGeoch and his associates (Johnson, 1933, McGeoch and McDonald, 1931, McGeoch and McGeoch, 1937) ran into direct conflict with his hypothesis and the experimental evidence supporting it. Using meaningful words, they consistently found that as the judged similarity of the original and interpolated materials increased, interference also increased. The highest degree of similarity they could obtain, where close synonyms appeared on the two serial lists, yielded the most interference. There was no evidence here of facilitation as one approached identity. In *The Psychology of Human Learning* (1942) McGeoch offered two alternative rapprochements between his data and the Skaggs-Robinson Hypothesis: (1) He distinguished "similarity of meaning" and "degrees of identity" as two different dimensions of similarity, each having a different interference function. This distinction was suggested by the fact that some of the experiments supporting the hypothesis (Harden, 1929, Kennelly, 1941, Robinson, 1927) had employed numeral and letter combinations with similarity indexed by the number of identical elements. Unfortunately, in other substantiating studies, materials were used in which identical elements were no more readily specifiable than with meaningful words. Dreis (1933), for example, used code-substitution, and Watson (1938) used card-sorting. Furthermore, this type of resolution implies an analysis of meaningful similarity that would segregate it from identity of elements, and this has not been done. (2) At a later point, McGeoch tried to resolve the difficulty by stating that his results applied only to the portion of the Robinson Curve between *B* and *C*, *i.e.*, that the maximum similarity of his materials only reached point *B*. However, given the multidirectional shape of this theoretical function and the fact that point *B* defines no degree of similarity, not only could any obtained data be fitted to some portion of it, but it could always be argued that the similarity of one's materials fell *anywhere* between *A* and *C*. In other words, this second suggestion is incapable of either proof or disproof.

Perhaps the clearest experimental evidence against either of McGeoch's resolutions appears in the results of a recent experiment by the writer (Osgood, 1946). *Also* using meaningful materials in the traditional retroaction paradigm, interference was found to *decrease* as the meaningful similarity among the response members increased. Not only would these results seem to fit "degrees of identity" rather than "similarity of meaning" as the functioning dimension, despite the nature of the materials used, but they fall within the A to B sector of the theoretical curve.

Quite apart from the apparent negative evidence in the McGeoch studies, the Skaggs-Robinson Hypothesis is inadequate on several grounds. It does, to be sure, allow ordinary learning to occur. But (1) it contains a dual function of facilitation in relation to similarity without specifying at what degree of similarity the shift occurs; (2) no specification is made of the locus of similarities within the materials practiced (whether among stimulus members, response members or both), and we have seen that both the direction and the degree of either transfer or retroaction are empirically predictable from such specification. One of the most recent attempts to integrate these data has been made by Gibson (1940). She followed Wylie's lead in differentiating between stimulus variation and response variation, and she added to this picture the refinement of stimulus generalization, derived from Pavlovian conditioning principles. Gibson's two theoretical laws were: (1) if responses are *identical* facilitation is obtained, its amount increasing with the degree of stimulus generalization (similarity); (2) if responses are *different* interference is obtained, its amount increasing with the degree of stimulus generalization (similarity). These hypotheses fit much of the data in the field and further serve to integrate the phenomena of human learning with those of the animal laboratory. But they are insufficient. (1) No account is given of the *degree* of response similarity, and this appears as one of the relevant variables. (2) We have one function (increasing interference) when responses are different and another (decreasing interference) when responses are "identical"; and one would anticipate, therefore, a strange, abrupt shift in function somewhere along the line as the degree of response difference is reduced. (3) The fundamental paradox remains: responses can never be truly identical but must always be different to some degree, yet ordinary learning can occur.

THE TRANSFER AND RETROACTION SURFACE

The formulation proposed here makes full use of Gibson's analysis, but, utilizing data which have recently become available, goes beyond it. It is quite literally constructed from the empirical laws presented above, and this can be demonstrated by use of Figure 3,

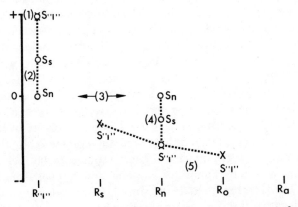

FIGURE 3. Allocation of experimental data: vertical, direction and degree of either transfer or retroaction; horizontal, degrees of response similarity. Numbers in parentheses refer to step in analysis followed in text.

which provides a rational framework within which the data can be integrated. The vertical dimension represents the direction and degree of *either* transfer or retroaction; degrees of response similarity are distributed along the horizontal dimension. The parenthetical numbers refer to the sequence of steps to be followed in allocating the data.

Let us first consider the ordinary learning of an association, the case in which the same materials are used for original and interpolated activities. Here functionally identical stimuli and responses are successively repeated and maximal facilitation is obtained, allowing us to locate the first point as shown (number *1*). The phenomena of positive transfer (stimulus generalization) and retroactive facilitation when responses are identical and stimuli varied are represented by the series of open circles (number *2*): as the degree of stimulus similarity decreases from "identity" less and less facilitation is obtained, effects of zero magnitude being found when stimuli are neutral. Data reported by Hovland (1937) and Hamilton (1943) are typical. As pointed out earlier, the fact that Hamilton and Gibson (1941) used the same materials and procedures, with the single exception that responses were the same in the former case and different in the latter, provides an extremely useful comparison (see number 3); where stimulus members are neutral, effects of approximately zero magnitude are obtained in both experiments, allowing us to link the Gibson and Hamilton data together on the zero-effect base line. In other words, variations in the relation between response members are of no consequence when stimulus members are completely unrelated. The Gibson experiment itself, along with other substantiating studies, provides data for the condition in which responses are different and neutral while stimulus similarity is varied. Here negative transfer and retroactive interference are regularly obtained, increasing in magnitude as the similarity of the stimulus members increases, and these data are represented by the series of solid circles (see number 4). There remains to be included the condition in which stimuli are constant and response similarity is varied. The fact that "identity" of stimulus and variation of response yields negative transfer and retroactive interference is amply testified to by a number of studies (Bruce, 1933, Gibson, 1941, Underwood, 1945). Experiments in which the *degree* of response similarity is systematically varied, as those by Bruce (1933) and Osgood (1946), show that interference is *less* for similar responses than for neutral ones. Since the latter study included a condition in which responses were neutral and stimuli functionally identical, thus matching the final point of the Gibson data, it is possible to link the two sets of facts together. These data are represented by the connected series of X's (number 5).

The pattern of empirical points established here sharply limits the possible theoretical functions that can be generated. By visually tracing the series of X's, for example, including the point for ordinary learning, a fairly well-defined curve becomes apparent, this curve representing the function for stimulus "identity." A family of such stimulus-relation curves has been constructed to fit both these empirical points and the requirements of common sense, and they appear in Figure 4. The function for *stimulus neutrality* is a straight line of zero effect, reflecting the reasonable fact that response variations are of no consequence when successive stimulus situations are completely unrelated. Given this as a zero-effect base line, increasing the similarity among stimuli yields a progressive maximization of *both* facilitation and interference, the actual direction of the effect being dependent upon response relations. The greatest facilitation and the greatest interference are possible only with functional *stimulus identity*. Intermediate transfer and retroaction effects fall be-

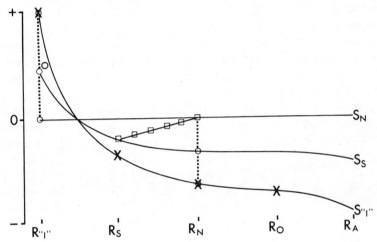

FIGURE 4. Family of stimulus-relation curves constructed from data in Figure 3; series of open squares represents data obtained by McGeoch and his associates (see text).

tween these limits depending upon degrees of stimulus similarity. The points for antagonistic responses, showing a final, sharp increase in interference, are admittedly hypothetical. However, the writer has recently reported (Osgood, 1948) evidence for a special form of *reciprocal inhibition* associated with the successive learning of meaningfully opposed responses. The assumption is made here that this inhibitory effect is maximal when responses are directly antagonistic.

But how do the classic findings of McGeoch and his associates fit this hypothesis? In a real sense, they serve as a crucial test of it, being both well substantiated and in apparent conflict with other results. It will be remembered that these investigators employed a method wherein the similarity of *both* stimuli and responses varied simultaneously and through the same degrees, actually from neutrality of both to high similarity (but not identity) of both. As may be seen from the row of open squares in Figure 4, the present hypothesis *must* predict gradually increasing amounts of interference under these conditions, and this is precisely the result obtained in these studies.

Although Figure 4 provides a useful method of demonstrating the congruence of empirical data and theoretical functions, it does not offer a clear picture of the hypothesis as a whole. To do so requires a three dimensional form, representing stimulus similarity, response similarity and degree of effect as simultaneously interrelated variables. Figure 5 presents what may be termed *the transfer and retroaction surface*. The vertical dimension represents the direction and degree of either transfer or retrocation, both having been shown to have identical functions of similarity; the width of the form represents stimulus similarity, from functional identity to neutrality; its length represents response similarity, varying from

THE TRANSFER AND RETROACTION SURFACE

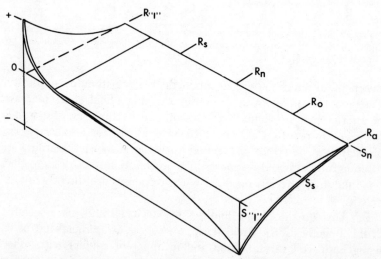

FIGURE 5. The transfer and retroaction surface: medial plane represents effects of zero magnitude; response relations distributed along length of solid and stimulus relations along its width.

functional identity, through neutrality, to direct antagonism. The median horizontal plane indicates effects of zero magnitude, and it may be seen that the condition of stimulus neutrality is co-extensive with this plane regardless of response variations while the remainder of the surface intersects this plane at a point between response "identity" and response similarity. Finally, it is apparent that we have here a smooth, unbroken sequence of transfer and retroaction functions, facilitative relations rising above the median plane and interfering relations falling below it. There are no reversals in these functions nor any abrupt shifts between identity and similarity. Identity becomes merely the limiting case of maximal similarity.

CERTAIN ADVANTAGES OF THIS HYPOTHESIS

By way of summary, certain advantages which this hypothesis offers in comparison with those which have preceded it may be indicated.

1. *All existing empirical data in the field are consistent with it and find representation upon the transfer and retroaction surface.* This statement is by necessity limited to those data wherein the locus of the similarities is specifiable and also by the adequacy of the writer's survey of the literature. The first limitation is not a serious one. If results can be shown to be lawful, and hence predictable, when such specification of the similarity relations is possible, the conflicting and confused results obtained under unspecifiable conditions are presumably attributable to unanalyzable variations in the paradigms employed. Witness the conclusive inconclusiveness on the question of formal discipline! This state of affairs illustrates why it is so difficult to make recommendations for efficient human learning in practical situations. What, for example, are the loci of similarities when the student simultaneously studies French and Spanish?

2. *The phenomena of both transfer and retroaction are integrated within a single framework, in so far as the similarity variable is concerned.* It is common textbook procedure to study transfer under learning and retroaction under forgetting, as if these processes were somehow different in kind. The present analysis, it is felt, is a step in the direction of integrating the problems of human learning. Another step in the same direction is also suggested here: distinctions

are often made in terms of meaningful vs. nonsense materials, meaningful similarity vs. degrees of identity, and so on. It should be pointed out that data substantiating each of the three empirical laws derived above have been obtained with meaningful and nonsense materials, with materials varying in terms of meaningful similarity as well as degrees of identity. There is here, of course, the underlying problem of defining similarity. It may be defined operationally in terms of generalization (*cf.* Gibson, 1940), although this definition is inherently circular since the phenomenon of generalization is nothing other than a case of positive transfer with functionally identical responses. Any precise behavioral definition of similarity will require much more knowledge of the nervous system than we have at present. In practice, degrees of similarity have been specified informally by experimenters or formally by a sample of judges, which probably suffices for our present rather gross purposes.

3. *Although constructed directly from existing empirical evidence, this hypothesis does go considerably beyond it, predicting phenomena that have not as yet been observed.* For one thing that portion of the transfer and retroaction surface where increasing similarity of response (high degrees) is accompanied by increasing facilitation remains to be explored by standard procedures, the Robinson group of studies having used a memory span technique.[1] It will also be noticed that the theoretical surface requires that, regardless of the degree of stimulus similarity, all functions must become facilitative at precisely the same degree of response similarity, somewhere between identity and high similarity. In other words, just as the degree of response variation is inconsequential when stimulus members are neutral, so there must exist (according to this hypothesis) some definite degree of response similarity for which all variations among stimuli will yield zero effect. This is a novel but necessary prediction from theory that sets an intriguing experimental problem. It is not inconceivable that this common shift over from facilitation to interference at a certain degree of variation among responses may reflect a basic characteristic of the nervous system—but this is all assuming

[1] An as yet uncompleted investigation by Mark W. Harriman at Johns Hopkins University appears to be filling in this gap in our empirical knowledge. With functionally identical stimulus members, responses on original and interpolated lists are varied by extremely small degrees, such as having the singular and plural of the same word on two lists, and the predicted results seem to be forthcoming.

that the present hypothesis will be found valid in terms of constantly accruing facts.

4. Finally, *this hypothesis resolves the fundamental paradox with which this paper began—the fact of ordinary learning becomes theoretically feasible.* The transfer and retroaction surface describes a system of curves within which the condition of ordinary learning, with functionally identical stimuli and responses in the materials successively practiced, is continuous with other relations. Identity is here merely the limiting case of maximal similarity, and no abrupt shifts of function are required to account for the fact that learning occurs.

[3]
The Formation of Learning Sets [1, 2]

HARRY F. HARLOW

In most psychological ivory towers there will be found an animal laboratory. The scientists who live there think of themselves as theoretical psychologists, since they obviously have no other rationalization to explain their extravagantly paid and idyllic sinecures. These theoretical psychologists have one great advantage over those psychological citizens who study men and women. The theoreticians can subject their subhuman animals, be they rats, dogs, or monkeys, to more rigorous controls than can ordinarily be exerted over human beings. The obligation of the thoretical psychologist is to discover general laws of behavior applicable to mice, monkeys, and men. In this obligation the theoretical psychologist has often failed. His deductions frequently have had no generality beyond the species

[1] This paper was presented as the presidential address of the Midwestern Psychological Association meetings in St. Paul, May 7, 1948.

[2] The researches described in this paper were supported in part by grants from the Special Research Fund of the University of Wisconsin for 1944–48.

SOURCE: H. F. Harlow, "The Formation of Learning Sets," *The Psychological Review*, 1949, **56**, 51–65. Reprinted by permission of H. F. Harlow and the American Psychological Association.

which he has studied, and his laws have been so limited that attempts to apply them to man have resulted in confusion rather than clarification.

One limitation of many experiments on subhuman animals is the brief period of time the subjects have been studied. In the typical problem, 48 rats are arranged in groups to test the effect of three different intensities of stimulation operating in conjunction with two different motivational conditions upon the formation of *an isolated* conditioned response. A brilliant Blitzkrieg research is effected—the controls are perfect, the results are important, and the rats are dead.

If this *do and die* technique were applied widely in investigations with human subjects, the results would be appalling. But of equal concern to the psychologist should be the fact that the derived general laws would be extremely limited in their application. There are experiments in which the use of naive subjects is justified, but the psychological compulsion to follow this design indicates that frequently the naive animals are to be found on both sides of the one-way vision screen.

The variety of learning situations that play an important rôle in determining our basic personality characteristics and in changing some of us into thinking animals are repeated many times in similar form. The behavior of the human being is not to be understood in terms of the results of single learning situations but rather in terms of the changes which are affected through multiple, though comparable, learning problems. Our emotional, personal, and intellectual characteristics are not the mere algebraic summation of a near infinity of stimulus-response bonds. The learning of primary importance to the primates, at least, is the formation of learning sets; it is the *learning how to learn efficiently* in the situations the animal frequently encounters. This learning to learn transforms the organism from a creature that adapts to a changing environment by trial and error to one that adapts by seeming hypothesis and insight.

The rat psychologists have largely ignored this fundamental aspect of learning and, as a result, this theoretical domain remains a *terra incognita*. If learning sets are the mechanisms which, in part, transform the organism from a conditioned response robot to a reasonably rational creature, it may be thought that the mechanisms are too intangible for proper quantification. Any such presupposition is false. It is the purpose of this paper to demonstrate the extremely orderly and quantifiable nature of the development of certain learning sets and, more broadly, to indicate the importance of learning sets to the development of intellectual organization and personality structure.

The apparatus used throughout the studies subsequently referred to is illustrated in Figure 1. The monkey responds by displacing one

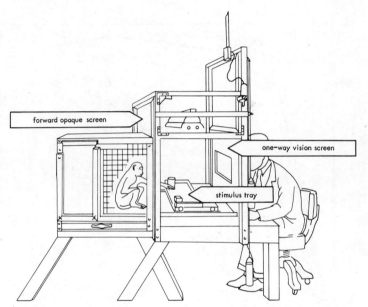

FIGURE 1. Wisconsin general test apparatus.

of two stimulus-objects covering the food-wells in the tray before him. An opaque screen is interposed between the monkey and the stimulus situation between trials and a one-way vision screen separates monkey and man during trials.

The first problem chosen for the investigation of learning sets was the object-quality discrimination learning problem. The monkey was required to choose the rewarded one of two objects differing in multiple characteristics and shifting in the left-right positions in a predetermined balanced order. A series of 344 such problems using 344 different pairs of stimuli was run on a group of eight monkeys. Each of the first 32 problems was run for 50 trials; the next 200 problems for six trials; and the last 112 problems for an average of nine trials.

In Figure 2 are presented learning curves which show the per cent of correct responses on the first six trials of these discriminations. The data for the first 32 discriminations are grouped for blocks of eight problems, and the remaining discriminations are arranged in blocks of 100, 100, 56, and 56 problems. The data indicate that

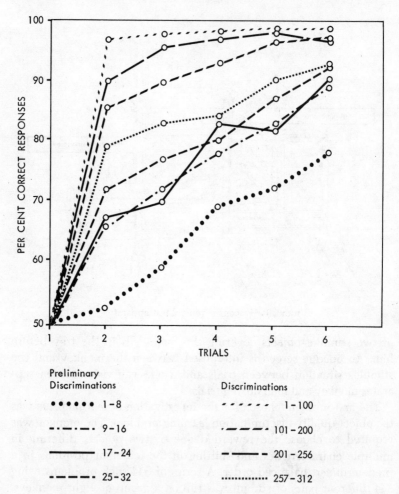

FIGURE 2. Discrimination learning curves on successive blocks of problems.

the subjects progressively improve in their ability to learn object-quality discrimination problems. The monkeys *learn how to learn* individual problems with a minimum of errors. It is this *learning how to learn a kind of problem* that we designate by the term *learning set*.

The very form of the learning curve changes as learning sets become more efficient. The form of the learning curve for the first eight discrimination problems appears S-shaped: it could be described as a curve of "trial-and-error" learning. The curve for the last 56 problems approaches linearity after Trial 2. Curves of similar form have been described as indicators of 'insightful' learning.

We wish to emphasize that this *learning to learn, this transfer from problem to problem* which we call the formation of a learning set, is a highly *predictable, orderly* process which can be demonstrated as long as controls are maintained over the subjects' experience and the difficulty of the problems. Our subjects, when they started these researches, had no previous laboratory learning experience. Their entire discrimination learning set history was obtained in this study. The stimulus pairs employed had been arranged and their serial order determined from tables of random numbers. Like non-sense syllables, the stimulus pairs were equated for difficulty. It is unlikely that any group of problems differed significantly in intrinsic difficulty from any other group.

In a conventional learning curve we plot change of performance over a series of *trials;* in a learning set curve we plot change in performance over a series of *problems*. It is important to remember that *we measure learning set in terms of problems* just as *we measure habit in terms of trials.*

Figure 3 presents a discrimination learning set curve showing progressive increase in the per cent of correct responses on Trials 2–6 on successive blocks of problems. This curve appears to be negatively accelerated or possibly linear.

Discrimination learning set curves obtained on four additional naive normal monkeys and eight naive monkeys with extensive unilateral cortical lesions, are shown in Figure 4. Brain-injured as well as normal monkeys are seen to form effective discrimination learning sets, although the partial hemidecorticate monkeys are less efficient than the normal subjects. Improvement for both groups is progressive and the fluctuations that occur may be attributed to

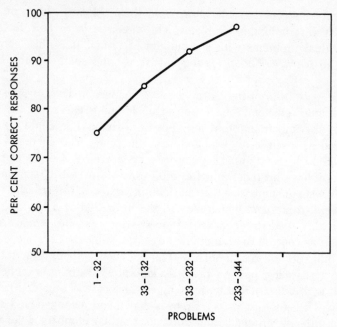

FIGURE 3. Discrimination learning set curve based on Trial 2–6 responses.

the small number of subjects and the relatively small number of problems, 14, included in each of the problem blocks presented on the abscissa.

Through the courtesy of Dr. Margaret Kuenne we have discrimination learning set data on another primate species. These animals were also run on a series of six-trial discrimination problems but under slightly different conditions. Macaroni beads and toys were substituted for food rewards, and the subjects were tested sans iron-barred cages. The data for these 17 children, whose ages range from two to five years and whose intelligence quotients range from 109 to 151, are presented in Figure 5. Learning set curves are plotted for groups of children attaining a predetermined learning criterion within differing numbers of problem blocks. In spite of the small number of cases and the behavioral vagaries that are known to characterize this primate species, the learning set curves are orderly and lawful and show progressive increase in per cent of correct responses.

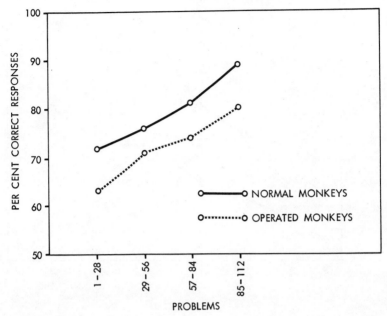

FIGURE 4. Discrimination learning set curves based on Trial 2–6 responses: normal and operated monkeys.

Learning set curves, like learning curves, can be plotted in terms of correct responses or errors, in terms of responses on any trial or total trials. A measure which we have frequently used is per cent of correct Trial 2 responses—the behavioral measure of the amount learned on Trial 1.

Figure 6 shows learning set curves measured in terms of the per cent correct Trial 2 responses for the 344-problem series. The data from the first 32 preliminary discriminations and the 312 subsequent discriminations have been plotted separately. As one might expect, these learning set curves are similar to those that have been previously presented. What the curves show with especial clarity is the almost unbelievable change which has taken place in the *effectiveness of the first training trial.* In the initial eight discriminations, this single paired stimulus presentation brings the Trial 2 performance of the monkeys to a level less than three per cent above chance; in the last 56 discriminations, this first training trial brings the performance of the monkeys to a level *less than three per cent* short

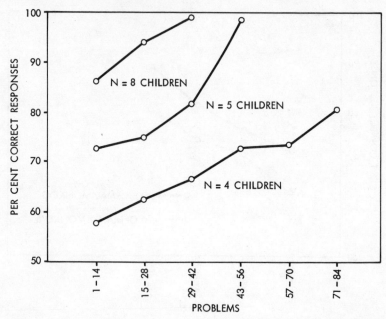

Figure 5. Discrimination learning set curves based on Trial 2–6 responses: children.

of perfection. Before the formation of a discrimination learning set, a single training trial produces negligible gain; after the formation of a discrimination learning set, *a single training trial constitutes problem solution.* These data clearly show that *animals can gradually learn insight.*

In the final phase of our discrimination series with monkeys there were subjects that solved from 20 to 30 consecutive problems with no errors whatsoever following the first blind trial—and many of the children, after the first day or two of training, did as well or better.

These data indicate the function of learning set in converting a problem which is initially difficult for a subject into a problem which is so simple as to be immediately solvable. The learning set is the mechanism that changes the problem from an intellectual tribulation into an intellectual triviality and leaves the organism free to attack problems of another hierarchy of difficulty.

For the analysis of learning sets in monkeys on a problem that is

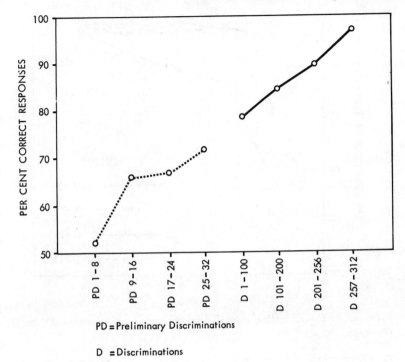

PD = Preliminary Discriminations

D = Discriminations

FIGURE 6. Discrimination learning set curve based on Trial 2 responses.

ostensibly at a more complex level than the discrimination problem, we chose the discrimination reversal problem. The procedure was to run the monkeys on a discrimination problem for 7, 9, or 11 trials and then to reverse the reward value of the stimuli for eight trials; that is to say, the stimulus previously correct was made incorrect and the stimulus previously incorrect became correct.

The eight monkeys previously trained on discrimination learning were tested on a series of 112 discrimination reversal problems. Discrimination reversal learning curves for successive blocks of 28 problems are shown in Figure 7. The measure used is per cent of correct responses on Reversal Trials 2 to 6. Figure 8 presents data on the formation of the discrimination reversal learning set in terms of the per cent of correct responses on Reversal Trial 2 for successive blocks of 14 problems. Reversal Trial 2 is the first trial following the "informing" trial, *i.e.*, the initial trial reversing the reward value

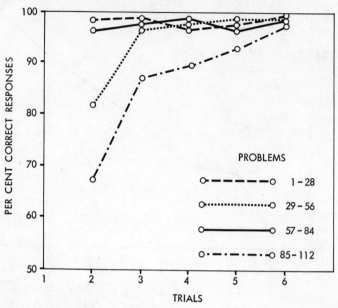

FIGURE 7. Discrimination reversal learning curves on successive blocks of problems.

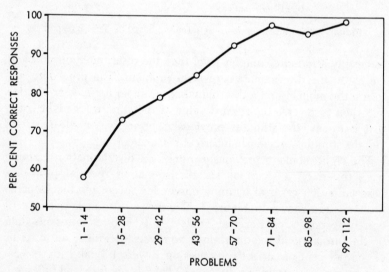

FIGURE 8. Discrimination reversal learning set curve based on Trial 2 responses.

of the stimuli. Reversal Trial 2 is the measure of the effectiveness with which the single informing trial leads the subject to abandon a reaction pattern which has proved correct for 7 to 11 trials, and to initiate a new reaction pattern to the stimulus pair. On the last 42 discrimination reversal problems the monkeys were responding as efficiently on Reversal Trial 2 as they were on complementary Discrimination Trial 2, *i.e.*, they were making over 97 per cent correct responses on both aspects of the problems. The eight monkeys made from 12 to 57 successive correct second trial reversal responses. Thus it becomes perfectly obvious that at the end of this problem the monkeys possessed sets both to learn and to reverse a reaction tendency, and that this behavior could be consistently and immediately elicited with hypothesis-like efficiency.

This terminal performance level is likely to focus undue attention on the one-trial learning at the expense of the earlier, less efficient performance levels. It should be kept in mind that this one-trial learning appeared only as the end result of an orderly and progressive learning process; insofar as these subjects are concerned, the insights are only to be understood in an historical perspective.

Although the discrimination reversal problems might be expected to be more difficult for the monkeys than discrimination problems, the data of Figure 9 indicate that the discrimination reversal learning set was formed more rapidly than the previously acquired discrimination learning set. The explanation probably lies in the nature of the transfer of training from the discrimination learning to the discrimination reversal problems. A detailed analysis of the discrimination learning data indicates the operation throughout the learning series of certain error-producing factors, but with each successive block of problems the frequencies of errors attributable to these factors are progressively decreased, although at different rates and to different degrees. The process might be conceived of as a learning of response tendencies that counteract the error-producing factors. A description of the reduction of the error-producing factors is beyond the scope of this paper, even though we are of the opinion that this type of analysis is basic to an adequate theory of discrimination learning.

Suffice it to say that there is a reason to believe that there is a large degree of transfer from the discrimination series to the reversal series, of the learned response tendencies counteracting the operation of two of the three primary error-producing factors thus far identified.

The combined discrimination and discrimination reversal data show clearly how the learning set delivers the animal from Thorndikian bondage. By the time the monkey has run 232 discriminations and followed these by 112 discriminations and reversals, he does

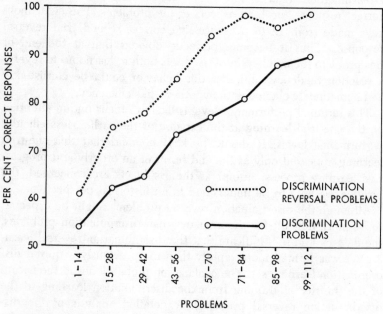

FIGURE 9. Discrimination reversal and discrimination learning set curves based on Trial 2 responses.

not possess 344 or 456 specific habits, bonds, connections or associations. We doubt if our monkeys at this time could respond with much more than chance efficiency on the first trial of any series of the previously learned problems. But the monkey does have a generalized ability to learn *any* discrimination problem or *any* discrimination reversal problem with the greatest of ease. Training on several hundred specific problems has not turned the monkey into an automaton exhibiting forced, stereotyped, reflex responses to specific stimuli. These several hundred habits have, instead, made the monkey an adjustable creature with an *increased capacity* to adapt to the ever-changing demands of a psychology laboratory environment.

We believe that other learning sets acquired in and appropriate to the monkey's natural environment would enable him to adapt better to the changing conditions there. We are certain, moreover, that learning sets acquired by man in and appropriate to his environment have accounted for his ability to adapt and survive.

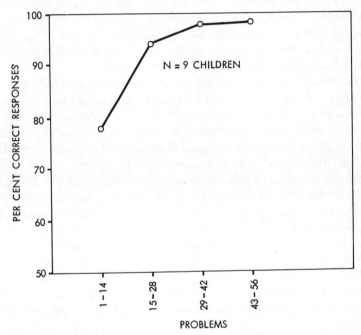

FIGURE 10. Discrimination reversal learning set curve based on Trial 2 responses: children.

Before leaving the problem of discrimination reversal learning we submit one additional set of data that we feel merits attention. Nine of the children previously referred to were also subjected to a series of discrimination reversal problems. The outcome is partially indicated in Figure 10 which shows the per cent of correct Reversal Trial 2 responses made on successive blocks of 14 problems. It can be seen that these three to five-year-old children clearly bested the monkeys in performance on this series of problems. Trial 2 responses approach perfection in the second block of 14 discrimination reversal problems. Actually, over half of the total Trial 2 errors were made by one child.

These discrimination reversal data on the children are the perfect illustration of set formation and transfer producing adaptable abilities rather than specific bonds. Without benefit of the monkey's discrimination reversal set learning curves we might be tempted to assume that the children's data indicate a gulf between human and subhuman learning. But the *extremely rapid* learning on the part the children is not unlike the *rapid* learning on the part of the monkeys, and analysis of the error-producing factors shows that the same basic mechanisms are operating in both species.

Following the discrimination reversal problem the eight monkeys were presented a new series of 56 problems designed to elicit alternation of unequivocally antagonistic response patterns. The first 7, 9, or 11 trials of each problem were simple object-quality discrimination trials. These were followed immediately by ten right-position discrimination trials with the same stimuli continuing to shift in the right-left positions in predetermined orders. In the first 7 to 11 trials, a particular object was correct regardless of its position. In the subsequent 10 trials, a particular position—the experimenter's right position—was correct, regardless of the object placed there. Thus to solve the problem the animal had to respond to object-quality cues and disregard position cues in the first 7 to 11 trials and, following the failure of reward of the previously rewarded object, he had to disregard object-quality cues and respond to position cues.

The learning data on these two antagonistic tasks are presented in Figure 11. It is to be noted that the object-quality curve, which is based on Trials 1 to 7, begins at a very high level of accuracy, whereas the position curve, plotted for Trials 1 to 10, begins at a level little above chance. This no doubt reflects the operation of the previously well-established object-quality discrimination learning set. As the series continues, the object-quality curve shows a drop until the last block of problems, while the position curve rises progressively. In the evaluation of these data, it should be noted that chance performance is 50 per cent correct responses for the object quality discriminations and 45 per cent for the position discriminations, since each sequence of 10 position trials includes an error "informing" trial. It would appear that the learning of the right-position discriminations interferes with the learning of the object-quality discriminations to some extent. In spite of this decrement in object-quality discrimination performance for a time, the subjects were functioning at levels far beyond chance on the antagonistic parts of the problems during the last half of the series. We believe that this behavior reflects the formation of a right-position learning set which operates at a high degree of independence of the previously established object-quality discrimination learning set.

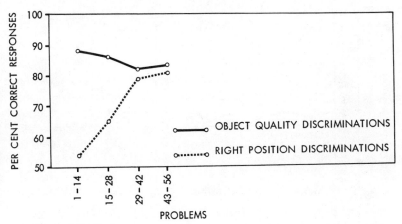

FIGURE 11. Learning set curves for problem requiring shift from object-quality discrimination to right-position discrimination.

The precision of the independent operation of these learning sets throughout the last 14 problems is indicated in Figure 12. Since the right-position part of the problem was almost invariably initiated by an error trial, these data are limited to those problems on which the first trial object-quality discrimination response was incorrect. The per cent of correct Trial 7 responses to the "A" object, the correct stimulus for the object-quality discriminations, is 98. The initiating error trial which occurs when the problem shifts without warning to a right- position problem, drops this per cent response to the "A" object to 52—a level barely above chance. The per cent of Trial 7 responses to the right position during the object-quality discriminations is 52. The single error trial initiating the shift of the problem to a right-position discrimination is followed by 97 per cent right-position responses on the next trial. In other words, *it is as though* the outcome of a single *push of an object* is adequate to switch off the "A"-object choice reaction tendency and to switch on the right-position choice reaction tendency.

The cue afforded by a single trial produces at this point almost complete discontinuity of the learning process. The only question now left unsettled in the controversy over hypotheses in subhuman animals is whether or not to use this term to describe the behavior of a species incapable of verbalization.

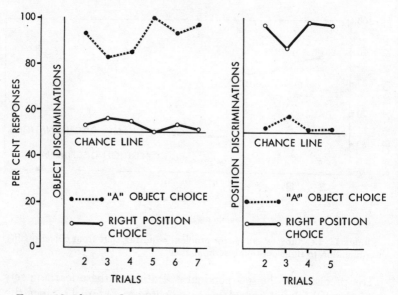

FIGURE 12. Object and position choices following initial errors on both phases of object-position shift series, based on problems 42–56.

Again, it should be remembered that both the object-quality discrimination learning set and the right-position discrimination learning set developed in a gradual and orderly manner. Only after the learning sets are formed do these phenomena of discontinuity in learned behavior appear.

Further evidence for the integrity of learning sets is presented in an additional experiment. Six monkeys with object-quality discrimination learning experience, but without training on reversal problems or position discriminations, were given seven blocks of 14 problems each, starting with a block of 25-trial object-quality discriminations, followed by a block of 14 25-trial positional discriminations composed of right-position and left-position problems presented alternately. The remaining five blocks of problems continued the alternate presentation of 14 object-quality discrimination problems and 14 right-left positional discrimination problems. Figure 13 presents

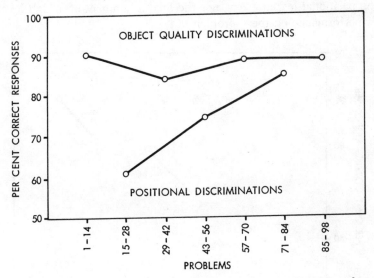

FIGURE 13. Learning set curves for problem series with alternating object-quality and positional discriminations, based on total trial responses.

curves showing the per cent of correct responses on total trials on these alternate blocks of antagonistic discriminations. The complex positional discrimination learning set curve shows progressive improvement throughout the series, whereas the object-quality discrimination curve begins at a high-level of accuracy, shows decrement on the second block, and subsequently recovers. By the end of the experiment the two basically antagonistic learning sets had "learned" to live together with a minimum of conflict. These data are the more striking if it is recalled that between each two blocks of object-quality discriminations there were 350 trials in which no object was differentially rewarded, and between each two blocks of 14 positional discriminations there were 350 trials in which no position was differentially rewarded.

In Figure 14 we present additional total-trial data on the formation of the positional learning set. These data show the change in performance on the first and last seven positional discriminations in each of the three separate blocks of positional discriminations. The interposed object-quality discrimination problems clearly produced interference, but they did not prevent the orderly development of the positional learning sets, nor the final attainment of a high level of performance on these problems.

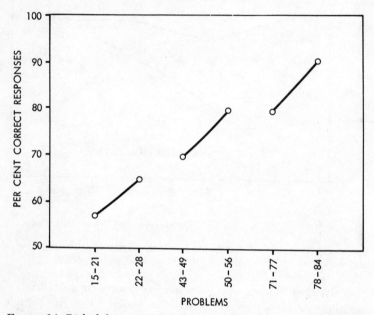

FIGURE 14. Right-left positional discrimination learning set curve based on total trial responses. (Data on antagonistic object-quality discrimination problems omitted.)

We have data which suggest that the educated man can face arteriosclerosis with confidence, if the results on brain-injured animals are applicable to men. Figure 15 shows discrimination learning set curves for the previously described groups of four normal monkeys and eight monkeys with very extensive unilateral cortical injury. The upper curves show total errors on an intial series of 112 six-trial discriminations. The lower curves show total errors on an additional group of 56 discriminations presented one year later. In both situations the full-brained monkeys make significantly better scores, but one should note that the educated hemidecorticate animals are superior to the uneducated unoperated monkeys. Such data suggest that half a brain is better than one if you compare the individuals having appropriate learning sets with the individuals lacking them.

More seriously, these data may indicate why educated people show less apparent deterioration with advancing age than unedu-

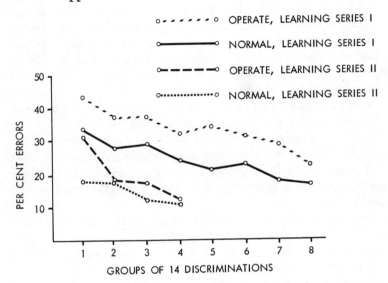

FIGURE 15. Discrimination learning set curves based on total error responses: normal and operated monkeys.

cated individuals, and the data lend support to the clinical observation that our fields of greatest proficiency are the last to suffer gross deterioration.

Although our objective data are limited to the formation of learning sets which operate to give efficient performance on intellectual problems, we have observational data of a qualitative nature on social-emotional changes in our animals. When the monkeys come to us they are wild and intractable but within a few years they have acquired, from the experimenter's point of view, good personalities. Actually we believe that one of the very important factors in the development of the good personalities of our monkeys is the formation of social-emotional learning sets organized in a manner comparable with the intellectual learning sets we have previously described. Each contact the monkey has with a human being represents a single specific learning trial. Each person represents a separate problem. Learning to react favorably to one person is followed by learning favorable reactions more rapidly to the next person to whom the monkey is socially introduced. Experience with additional individuals enables the monkey to learn further how to behave with human beings, and eventually the monkey's favorable reactions to new people are acquired so rapidly as to appear almost instantaneous.

The formation of social-emotional learning sets is not to be confused with mere stimulus generalization, a construct applied in this field with undue freedom. Actually a learning set once formed determines in large part the nature and direction of stimulus generalization. In the classic study in which Watson conditioned fear in Albert, the child developed a fear of the rat and generalized this fear, but failed to develop or generalize fear to Watson, even though Watson must have been the more conspicuous stimulus. Apparently Albert had already formed an affectional social-emotional learning set to people, which inhibited both learning and simple Pavlovian generalization.

Our observations on the formation of social-emotional learning sets have been entirely qualitative and informal, but there would appear to be no reason why they could not be studied experimentally.

The emphasis throughout this paper has been on the rôle of the historical or experience variable in learning behavior—the forgotten variable in current learning theory and research. Hull's Neo-behaviorists have constantly emphasized the necessity for an historical approach to learning, yet they have not exploited it fully. Their experimental manipulation of the experience variable has been largely limited to the development of isolated habits and their generalization. Their failure to find the phenomenon of discontinuity in learning may stem from their study of individual as opposed to repetitive learning situations.

The field theorists, unlike the Neo-behaviorists, have stressed insight and hypothesis in their description of learning. The impression these theorists give is that these phenomena are properties of the innate organization of the individual. If such phenomena appear independently of a gradual learning history, we have not found them in the primate order.

Psychologists working with human subjects have long believed in the phenomenon of learning sets and have even used sets as explanatory principles to account for perceptual selection and incidental learning. These psychologists have not, however, investigated the nature of these learning sets which their subjects bring to the experimental situation. The determining experiential variables of these learning sets lie buried in the subjects' pasts, but the development of such sets can be studied in the laboratory as long as the human race continues to reproduce its kind. Actually, detailed knowledge of the nature of the formation of learning sets could be of such importance to educational theory and practice as to justify prolonged and systematic investigation.

In the animal laboratory where the experiential factor can be easily controlled, we have carried out studies that outline the development and operation of specific learning sets. We believe that the construct of learning sets is of importance in the understanding of adaptive behavior. Since this is our faith, it is our hope that our limited data will be extended by those brave souls who study *real* men and *real* women.

[4]
Implicit Verbal Chaining in Paired-Associate Learning [1]

WALLACE A. RUSSELL and
LOWELL H. STORMS

The role of covert symbolic processes in behavior determination has been emphasized by many psychological theorists, but the rela-

[1] This study is part of a larger series of studies of verbal behavior being conducted at the University of Minnesota. The series is being sponsored by the Office of Naval Research (Contract No. N8 onr-66216) under its policy of encouraging basic research.

SOURCE: W. A. Russell and L. H. Storms, "Implicit Verbal Chaining in Paired-Associate Learning," *The Journal of Experimental Psychology*, 1955, **49**, 287–293. Reprinted by permission of W. A. Russell and the American Psychological Association.

tive lack of supporting experimental evidence for this influence has been noted by several writers (Bugelski and Scharlock, 1952, McGeoch and Irion, 1952, p. 110). Among the various factors deemed relevant to the operation of mediational or symbolic processes, the verbal habits of the individual have been prominently suggested. The work of Foley and Cofer (1943) on verbally mediated generalization, and of Bousfield (1953), Jenkins and Russell (1952), and others working with recall, have established that the influence of such verbal associations can be studied effectively under experimental conditions.

While the mediational role of word associations has been demonstrated in several performance situations, there are surprisingly few studies which report positive findings with regard to the effects of mediated associations upon learning. Bugelski and Scharlock, using paired-associate learning and nonsense syllables, have provided what they term a "reasonably clear-cut demonstration of mediated association in the learning of verbal material" (Bugelski and Scharlock, 1952, p. 337). Their Ss showed facilitated learning of A–C associates when another term, B, presumably intervened between A and C as a consequence of previous learning of associations A–B and B–C. The term B, then, provided an implicit common term which was elicited by A and which in turn tended to elicit C. This mediation of the correct response C occurred even though Ss did not report deliberate use of the common term as a mnemonic device. The Bugelski and Scharlock data provide a much clearer instance of mediation than did the earlier experiments of Peters (1935). Although the latter obtained some positive results, the majority of his test situations failed to demonstrate mediational effects.

Both Bugelski and Scharlock and Peters worked with associations learned within the context of the experiment and neither considered situations involving more than one intervening term. Nevertheless, applications of the mediation hypothesis have frequently referred to existing language habits and have almost always involved reference to a "chain" of several intervening terms which are linked on an associative basis. Uniprocess theorists who, according to Harlow (1951, p. 452), maintain that "thinking is dependent only upon the formation and appropriate elicitation of a vast number of simple associations" have most commonly assumed that (*a*) mediational effects can occur across several intervening terms, and (*b*) these influences are at least as strong for associations between real words as between nonsense syllables. Hull's concept of pure stimulus acts (Hull, 1931), Miller's extension of the notion of verbally mediated generalization (Miller, 1951, p. 181), and Osgood's discussion of thinking (Osgood, 1953, p. 638) are but a few examples in which one or the other of these assumptions has been made. However, neither Peters nor Bugelski and Scharlock provide a basis for these assumptions.

The purpose of this experiment was to test the adequacy of the above assumptions by observing the effects of mediating verbal processes on paired-associate learning when the mediating process is implemented in part by pre-existing language habits and extends over more than one implicit verbal term.

METHOD

Design

The design of this study was similar to that of Bugelski and Scharlock (1952). Their Ss learned three paired-associate lists: List 1 established A-B assocations; List 2, B-C associations; and List 3 tested for mediation effects in the learning of A-C associations. In the study reported here, real words were used rather than nonsense syllables, and two implicit terms rather than one linked the pairs learned on the test trials. Here, the learning of List 1 established A-B associations. The B term was in each case a stimulus word from the Kent-Rosanoff association test (Kent and Rosanoff, 1910). Recently obtained norms for responses on this test [2] then made it possible to infer certain B-C associations without establishing them experimentally. Similarly, other unpublished studies provided normative data concerning the most frequent associative responses (D) made to the C terms. Thus, once the A-B associations were learned, it was possible to infer an associative chain leading from A to B to C to D. The test for mediational effects was made by requiring Ss to learn a list containing A-D pairings, and appropriate control pairings (A-X) of non-chained terms. It was hypothesized that the A-D pairings would be learned more easily than the A-X pairings. The manner in which associative chains might facilitate the elicitation and learning of A-D pairs is schematically illustrated as follows:

[2] Revised norms for 100 words from the Kent-Rosanoff word-association test were obtained from 1008 students in beginning psychology classes at the University of Minnesota. This work was carried out as part of a larger project on verbal behavior. Information concerning these norms may be obtained from the authors.

<table>
<tr><td></td><td>List 1</td><td>Associations Inferred
from Norms</td><td>List 2 (Test List)</td></tr>
</table>

	List 1	*Associations Inferred from Norms*	*List 2 (Test List)*
Chaining Paradigm	$A_1\ldots > B_1$	$(B_1 \to C_1 \to D_1)$	$A_1 \ldots \ldots > D_1$
			$(B_1 \to C_1)$
Control Paradigm	$A_2 \ldots > B_2$	$(B_2 \to C_2 \to D_2)$	$A_2 \ldots \ldots \ldots > X_2$
			$(B_2 \to C_2 \to D_2)$

Broken arrows indicate the association to be learned in each list. Solid arrows represent associations established before a list is learned. It can be seen that associations existing before the learning of the test list provide an indirect linkage of the A and D terms which must become associated in the chaining paradigm. In the control paradigm, a similar linkage exists between A and D, but no such connection can be inferred between the A-X pairs which are to be learned.

Construction of paired-associate lists.—Tables 1 and 2 contain the associative frequencies from the norms [3] for the three most frequent responses to the words relevant to this experiment. Table 1 provides this information for the ten Kent-Rosanoff stimulus words employed and Table 2 provides analogous data for the most frequent responses to those ten words.

Table 3 contains the nonsense syllables, the particular associative chains, and the control words used throughout the experiment. List 1 (A-B pairings) was made up of the nonsense syllables in Column A and the corresponding words in Column B. Columns B, C, and D list the verbal associative chains $(B \to C \to D)$ derived from the normative tables. Two test lists were formed. One combined the first five nonsense syllables of Column A with the five corresponding words of Column D and the last five nonsense syllables with the corresponding words of Column X. The other combined the first five nonsense syllables in Column A with the five corresponding words of Column X and the last five nonsense syllables with the five corresponding words of Column D. Thus the two lists were counterbalanced and each contained five A-D and five A-X pairs. The response words of Form 1 of the test list are followed by a "1" in the table; the remaining words made up Form 2.

The ten nonsense syllables of Column A were selected from Melton (9), and all had Glaze association values of 0%. The ten verbal chains listed in Columns B, C, and D of the table were selected so that as far as the complete norms would indicate, no word in any chain appeared among the ten most frequent responses to any word in any other chain. In addition, no final word (D) in a chain appeared as a response to the first word (B) more than seven times in the 1008 responses to that word in the norms. It may be noted that while Column C is essential to the construction of the ten associative chains, no words in that column appeared in any of the experimental lists. The control words in Column X were chosen from the Kent-Rosanoff list such that none appeared

---

[3] See footnote 2.

among the ten most frequent responses to any of the chained words and no chained word appeared among the ten most frequent responses to a control word. Finally, the control words were matched with the final words of each chain on the basis of Thorndike-Lorge (1944) frequency as a partial equalization of difficulty between control and experimental words.

TABLE 1

Associative Frequencies of the Three Most Frequent Responses to Ten Kent-Rosanoff Stimulus Words
(Based on R's from 1008 Ss)

Stimulus	Primary R	f	Secondary R	f	Tertiary R	f
Stem	Flower	402	Plant	224	Leaf	125
Memory	Mind	119	Remember	99	Forget	80
Soldier	Army	187	Sailor	182	Man	101
Trouble	Bad	89	Shooter	49	Worry	45
Wish	Want	124	Dream	118	Desire	112
Justice	Peace	250	Law	182	Courts	163
Thief	Steal	286	Robber	138	Crook	69
Ocean	Water	314	Sea	233	Blue	111
Command	Order	196	Army	102	Obey	78
Fruit	Apple	378	Vegetable	114	Orange	94

Procedure

Twenty-seven sophomore women from a beginning psychology class served as Ss.

Following general instructions on paired-associate learning, each S learned List 1 on a standard Hull-type memory drum. Each stimulus word was exposed for 2 sec. before the response word appeared beside it for another 2-sec. period. The next stimulus word followed immediately, except that 4 sec. elapsed after each complete trial through the list. The S was required to learn the ten pairs in List 1 to a criterion of three consecutive trials in which all response words were correctly anticipated. To control for serial position effects, the list was presented in three successive random orders of pairs before the first order was repeated. Three Ss failed to reach the criterion on List 1 within 40 min. and were not used further in the experiment.

After a pause of 4 min., each remaining S was presented with either Form 1 or Form 2 of the test list. The Ss were instructed that the procedure was exactly the same as for List 1 and were urged to do their best on the test list. Since one S failed to reach the criterion of one trial in which

TABLE 2

**Associative Frequencies of the Three Most Frequent Responses
to Ten Primary Responses to Kent-Rosanoff Stimulus Words
(Based on R's from 100 Ss)**

Word	Primary R	f	Secondary R	f	Tertiary R	f
Flower	Smell	15	Rose	12	Pretty	12
Mind	Brain	15	Matter	14	Think ⎱ Soul ⎰	12
Army	Navy	39	Service	7	Soldier ⎱ Man ⎰	4
Bad	Good	71	Evil	4	Mean	3
Want	Need	27	Desire	19	Have	8
Peace	War	42	Dove	10	Quiet	8
Steal	Take	14	Thief	10	Rob	8
Water	Drink	19	Thirsty	14	Wet	11
Order	Disorder	14	Command	6	Stop	5
Apple	Tree	16	Red	14	Orange	13

TABLE 3

**Nonsense Syllables, Associative Chains,
and Control Words Used in Forming
the Paired-Associate Lists**

A	B	C	D	X
Non-sense Syllable	First Chained Word	Second Chained Word	Final Chained Word	Control Word
CEF	Stem	Flower	Smell (1)	Joy
DAX	Memory	Mind	Matter (1)	Afraid
YOV	Soldier	Army	Navy (1)	Cheese
VUX	Trouble	Bad	Good (1)	Music
WUB	Wish	Want	Need (1)	Table
GEX	Justice	Peace	War	House (1)
JID	Thief	Steal	Take	Sleep (1)
ZIL	Ocean	Water	Drink	Doctor (1)
LAJ	Command	Order	Disorder	Cabbage (1)
MYV	Fruit	Apple	Red	Hand (1)

Note.—The words and syllables were presented in capital letters exactly as above. The response words of Form 1 of the test list are followed by a "1."

all the response words were correctly anticipated, there remained 23 Ss for the final analysis of results. Twelve of these learned Form 1 of the test list and 11 learned Form 2.

For each S, all correct anticipations and errors were tabulated for both List 1 and the test list. Measures used in the final analysis were: (a) the number of trials required to reach the criterion on List 1; (b) the number of mediated (D) and unmediated (X) responses occurring in the first five different correct anticipations by each S; (c) the total number of correct responses made for the mediated (D) and unmediated (X) words during the test trials.

Control Experiment

Twelve additional female Ss from the same population were used in a subsequently performed control experiment designed to allow a comparison of the learning of A-D and A-X pairs in a situation where associative chaining could not differentially contribute to the learning of the pairs. Instead of learning List 1, these Ss first learned either Form 1 or Form 2 of the test list. The second list was the other form of the test list. Thus, in the control experiment, associative facilitation due to $A \rightarrow B \rightarrow C \rightarrow D$ linkages was not possible because the A-B associations of List 1 were not learned by any S. The analysis of results for the control Ss was based on measures similar to those of the main experiment.

RESULTS

Since two forms of the test list and two groups of Ss were involved in the design, the equivalence of the two lists and the two groups must be established before the combined results can be dealt with. An analysis of the mean number of trials required to reach the criterion of learning on List 1, which all Ss learned, indicated that the 12 Ss who subsequently learned Form 1 of the test list did not differ significantly ($t = .52$) from the 11 Ss who subsequently learned Form 2 of the test list. The mean for the former group was 25.00 ($SD = 9.17$); for the latter it was 22.91 ($SD = 9.30$). With respect to performance on the two forms of the test list, the mean number of correct anticipations per S during learning did not differ significantly between Forms 1 and 2. The means for Forms 1 and 2 were, respectively, 67.08 ($SD = 30.75$) and 58.09 ($SD = 17.04$). The Behrens-Fisher d of .87 did not allow rejection of the null hypothesis concerning form differences.

As a consequence of these comparisons, the results from Forms 1 and 2 of the test list were combined. In order to determine whether the response terms for A–D pairs, for which associative chaining was possible, were more easily elicited during the early trials, an analysis was made of the first five different correct responses made by each S. Of the 115 responses in this analysis, 67 were members of "chained" A–D pairs and 48 were from "unchained" A–X pairs. The normal curve approximation to the binomial indicates that a result this large and in this direction would occur by chance less than 4 times in 100 if the probabilities of successes for A–D and A–X pairs were equal. Of the 23 Ss in this part of the experiment, 19 showed more chained than unchained responses in their first five different correct responses. The same one-tailed binomial test indicated that this result would occur by chance only 1 time in 1000 if the probabilities of successes for all pairs were equal. The conclusion that chained words were more easily elicited during the early trials of learning seemed warranted.

The major purpose of the experiment, however, was to compare the ease with which chained and unchained pairs were learned. The design allowed this comparison to be made with each S acting as her own control. Since each S learned an equal number of chained (A–D) and unchained (A–X) pairs, the total number of correct anticipations by each S for the unchained pairs was subtracted from the corresponding total for chained pairs. If there is facilitation of the learning of chained pairs (i.e., S has a larger number of correct anticipations on the A–D than on the A–X pairs) this difference will be positive. Over all Ss the mean difference between chained and unchained pairs was 3.74 ($SD = 5.32$). A t of 3.30 ($.01 > p > .001$) leads to rejection of the null hypothesis, and the conclusion that there was facilitation of learning of A–D pairs as contrasted with the learning of A–X pairs.

A secondary analysis of performance on Form 1 and Form 2 separately revealed that the direction of the difference between chained and unchained pairs was positive for both forms (Form 1, $M = +4.92$, $SD = 5.85$; Form 2, $M = +2.45$, $SD = 4.31$). For Form 1, the t of 2.79 was significant at the .02 level of confidence. For Form 2, the t of 1.80 was between the .15 and .10 levels.

It was recognized that, if for reasons other than associative chaining, the A–D pairs were as a group intrinsically easier to learn than the A–X pairs, the results obtained here could be accounted for on the basis of that factor alone. The control study was run to pro-

TABLE 4

Summary of Major Results

Experiment	Initial Successful Anticipations (First 5 Different Correct R's for Each S)			Total Correct Responses: Mean of Chained Minus Unchained	
	Chained	Unchained	Signifi- cance of Difference	(3)	Significance
Main	67	48	.04	+3.74	.01
Control	30	30		−0.50	

vide information about the relative difficulty of A–D and A–X pairs in a situation where chaining of A–D pairs was not possible. The 12 Ss in the control experiment learned both Forms 1 and 2 of the test list. The performance of these Ss on whichever form was learned last provided the basis for the analysis of the control experiment. First, the mean number of correct anticipations of the response word was determined for the ten A–D and the ten A–X pairs. The means were 7.06 and 7.35 respectively, with SD's of 1.29 and 1.39. This difference did not approach significance and the direction of difference is unfavorable to the hypothesis that the A–D pairs were easier to learn than the A–X pairs. Finally, the two major analyses of the main experiment were repeated here. As Table 4 indicates, neither of the differences tested was significant, and in each case the direction of difference did not favor the A–D pairs. In the absence of the possibility of associative chaining, then, there was no evidence of easier learning of the A–D pairs used in this experiment.

DISCUSSION

Statistically, these results provide stronger evidence for mediational effects in learning than do the results of Bugelski and Scharlock (1952). This is true in spite of the fact that the present experiment involves one more step in the chain of associations mediating the facilitated learning. Instead of an A–B–C sequence contributing to the learning of A–C, an A–B–C–D chain contributed to the learning of A–D. This demonstration of mediational influences extending over more than one intervening term, and involving language habits established prior to the experiment, offers some confirmation for theoretical explanations of thinking, problem solving, etc., which have postulated the operation of such complex implicit associative sequences.

Of course, the highly significant results obtained here, in the face of less convincing evidence obtained in schematically simpler situations (Bugelski and Scharlock), raise the problem of accounting for this stronger effect. Two possibilities occur to the writers. First, it is probable that this experiment allowed a more efficient analysis by removing variability due to individual differences in learning ability. Although Bugelski and Scharlock endeavored to have each S act as his own control, their technique of analysis admittedly left some individual difference factors operating. Our procedure of using within individual differences removed this variable and may have allowed mediational effects to be revealed more sensitively. Furthermore, it is at least conceivable that the pre-existing verbal habits of this experiment were stronger than the associations learned during the Bugelski-Scharlock experiment. It is probable that such strong associations, if such they were, brought about mediational effects more readily than weaker associations would have done.

The mere demonstration of mediational influences in learning, however, does not explain how the effect is achieved. The most plausible explanation would hold that the presence of an associative chain between the stimulus term and the response term in paired-associate learning increases the probability that the response term will be elicited in the learning situation. Any such elicitation would presumably have two effects. First, it would increase the total number of correct responses made during learning. This would be a performance change influencing the criterion measures used in this study. Second, there would be an influence on learning. The performance change, of course, does not necessarily reflect a change in the underlying learning process itself. Nevertheless, such a learning change is implied, since any factor which increases the frequency of occurrence of a correct response would increase the number of reinforced trials and thus indirectly influence the amount of learning.

Less obvious is the possibility that the differences between the mediated and unmediated pairs are due to interference effects in the learning of the control (A–X) pairs. Although interference due to the tendency for the A terms to elicit B was controlled by the design, possible differential interference effects may be seen when the entire A–B–C–D sequence is considered. If the probability of the elicitation of D is enhanced by the presence of A, as is stated above, then this tendency would compete with the elicitation of the correct response X in the unmediated pairs and possibly delay learning. It is conceivable that the associative chains used here produced both a facilitative effect upon mediated pairs and an interference effect upon unmediated pairs. The possibility that these two effects of associative chains do operate is amenable to experimental test, although the design of this experiment and that of Bugelski and Scharlock (1952) do not allow an analysis which would separate them.

Whatever the explanation of the mediational effect may be, there can be little doubt that it is the phenomenon underlying the superior performance of Ss on the A–D pairs. The controls inherent in the main experiment plus the additional information from the control experiment leave little room for alternative hypotheses. Such factors as serial position, idiosyncrasies of words and Ss, etc. operated equally for the mediated and nonmediated pairs and could not account for the differences obtained.

The fact that questions following the experiment yielded no evidence that Ss could verbalize the mediating terms only emphasizes the Bugelski-Scharlock conclusion that mediated association may be "unconscious."

Summary

This experiment was designed to study the effects of mediating verbal processes on paired-associate learning when the mediating process is implemented in part by pre-existing language habits and extends over more than one implicit verbal term.

First, ten chains of word associations, B-C-D, were constructed from normative data on association frequencies. Twenty-three female college Ss then learned a list of A-B pairs where the A terms were nonsense syllables and the B terms were the initial members of the chains described above. The test situation required that Ss learn another list consisting of A-D and A-X pairs. The D terms were the final members of the associative word chains, and the X terms were not associated with any of the chains. A control experiment revealed that the A-D and A-X pairs did not differ in difficulty in the absence of chaining possibilities.

It was found that the A-D pairs were learned significantly faster, and elicited earlier in learning, than the A-X pairs. It was concluded that implicit verbal chains of more than one link mediated these effects. Reasons for these results being even more clear-cut than those of schematically simpler previous experiments were discussed.

[5]
Transfer After Training with Single Versus Multiple Tasks [1]

CARL P. DUNCAN

Studies of learning to learn (e.g., McGeoch, 1952) and learning set (e.g., Harlow, 1949) show clearly that performance improves during practice on a series of similar tasks. However, most such experiments have not compared performance on a transfer task of the group that had practiced on the series of tasks with another group that had been given the same total amount of practice on a single task. Because of this, it cannot be determined how much of the increasing positive transfer called learning to learn or learning set is due to experience with a variety of tasks and how much is due to amount of practice per se. Since positive transfer varies directly with amount of practice even on a single task (Underwood, 1950),

[1] This research was performed under Contract No. AF 33(616)-308 between Northwestern University and the Psychology Branch of the Aero Medical Laboratory, Directorate of Research, Wright Air Development Center. I am much indebted to the following people for supervisory work and for advice: Drs. Benton J. Underwood, Ross L. Morgan, Edward Schwartz, John C. Jahnke, and John W. Cotton. Space limitations prevent giving credit to the large group of people who assisted in collecting the data.

source: C. P. Duncan, "Transfer After Training with Single Versus Multiple Tasks," *The Journal of Experimental Psychology*, 1958, Vol. **55**, No. 1, pp. 63–72. Reprinted by permission of C. P. Duncan and the American Psychological Association.

it seems necessary to determine if anything is learned from practice on a series of tasks that is not learned from an equal amount of practice on one task. This is the problem of the present study.

A design in which at least two groups are given the same total amount of training, one on a single task (constant training), the other on a series of tasks (varied training), with both groups tested on the same transfer task, has apparently been used in only two previous studies. Dashiell (1924), using code substitution, found that during training the constant group (same code every day) showed considerable improvement in its one task, while the varied group (new code every day) improved only slightly. However, on transferring to a new code, the varied group performed better.

The most thorough study was done by Crafts (1927). In his several experiments he found that in all types of tasks varied training produced superior transfer only when some characteristic of a series of tasks remained unchanged ("common element") over all (including transfer) tasks, while other characteristics varied. When the common element was eliminated, varied training produced no better transfer.

In spite of Crafts' suggestion that varied training is advantageous only when common elements are present, Dashiell's findings indicate that some type of habit that facilitates positive transfer can be developed when there is only a general similarity among tasks. This approach, i.e., training with tasks having only a nonspecific similarity, is used in the present study.

In this paper varied training is treated as a continuum, with constant training as one extreme, because certain degrees of varied training may be advantageous while other degrees may not. Degree of varied training is here defined in terms of the number of tasks (variations) introduced during training.

The other major variable is the total amount of practice or training given. This variable is necessary, since if total practice were equal for all degrees of varied training, increasing the number of training tasks means decreasing the amount of practice on each. Since it is not known whether varied training can be treated in terms of variation per se, or whether there is an interaction between the number of variations and the amount of practice on each, total amount of practice, and therefore amount of practice on each training variation, will also be manipulated to permit testing for this interaction.

Method

Apparatus

The manipulandum, operated from a sitting position, was a lever, 24 in. long, the top, free end of which could be moved into any one of 13 slots cut 1 in. deep and 1 in. apart in a steel plate. The slots were arranged in a semicircle concave to S. A red jewel light was immediately above, a microswitch immediately below, each slot. Movement of the lever into any slot depressed the microswitch and flashed on the light above whichever slot was correct for the stimulus showing, thus informing S which slot was correct immediately after each response. The slots were also numbered from 1 to 13, from left to right, with a large numeral printed above each jewel light. Immediately above the lights and numerals was the aperture of a memory drum, the front surface of which fitted into a hole in a large screen which prevented S from seeing E or the rest of the apparatus.

Behind the screen E faced a panel of two rows of 13 lights each which were numbered in each row. The light on in the top row indicated to E which slot was correct at the moment; the light on in the bottom row indicated which slot S's lever had entered. Recording of correct and incorrect responses was done manually by E. A set of 13 telephone jacks permitted pairing of a set of stimuli with the slots in any order.

Tasks.—Since responses were always movements of the lever into slots, a task is defined as a set of 13 stimuli. Thus, varied training was accomplished primarily by training with different sets of stimuli (although it will be seen later that another method of varied training received some attention).

TABLE 1

Conditions of the Experiment
(Entries are the number of trials on each training task.)

Number of Training Tasks	Days of Training		
	2	5	10
10	4	10	20
5	8	20	40
2	20	50	100
1	40	100	200
10R	4	10	20
Total trials	40	100	200

There were 10 tasks used only during training, and two tasks used only during the two transfer tests. Each training task consisted of 13 relatively meaningless forms. Each stimulus form within a task was produced by drawing elaborations (surplus lines) on a single "theme" or basic figure, such as a circle, a letter, etc. A different theme was used for each task, thus no stimulus in any task had any obvious similarity to a stimulus in another task. Because of this, and because stimuli were assigned to slots haphazardly, it will be assumed that there was little or no transfer among tasks based on specific stimulus generalization.

Tasks used for the two transfer tests were: (*a*) H figures, 13 forms built on a theme (capital H) not used for any training task, and (*b*) nonsense syllables of low association value and low intratask similarity. Thus, transfer was tested both with a task (H figures) that had relatively high, and a task (nonsense syllables) that had relatively low, over-all similarity to the training tasks.

All sets of training and transfer stimuli were mounted on tapes cut to fit the memory drum. To prevent serial learning, the 13 stimuli in each task were mounted in 12 different orders in a single vertical column on the tape. Since the tape was an endless belt, there was no apparent beginning or end of a task. There were no rests between trials, but after every 39 stimulus presentations (three trials or three orders), a blank space on the tape appeared for 4 sec. The stimuli were machine paced, each appearing for 4 sec.

Conditions

Manipulation of the number-of-training tasks variable was accomplished by training different groups with 1, 2, 5, or 10 tasks. The 1-task condition is defined as constant training and can be considered the control for varied training provided by the 2-, 5-, and 10-task conditions. There is no control group for transfer per se, i.e., a group tested on transfer tasks without any training.

Amount of practice was varied by giving 2, 5, or 10 days of training at the rate of 20 trials per day. Thus, the 1-task group that was trained for 10 days received 200 training trials on its one task; the 10-task group trained for two days received only four trials on each task, etc. Conditions of the experiment, and number of trials on each training task for each condition, are shown in Table 1.

The Re-Paired Task Condition

When Ss are trained with different sets of stimuli they not only receive practice with a greater variety of stimuli than do Ss in the constant-training condition, but they also receive more practice at starting from scratch and gradually acquiring S-R associations. As a partial check on the importance of this factor, i.e., experience at forming new associations, another method of varied training was employed in which only one set of stimuli was used throughout training and different "tasks" were provided by re-pairing the stimuli with the slots in completely different combinations. The only re-paired-task groups run (indicated by the row labeled 10R in Table 1) were three (with 2, 5, or 10 days of training) that were trained with 10 completely different re-pairings of the stimuli and responses.

Notation

Each of the 15 groups indicated in Table 1 will be denoted by two numbers, the first number indicating number of days of training, the second indicating number of training tasks, thus, Group 10–10, Group 5–10R, etc.

Assignment of Training Tasks

Each S in the three 1-task and the three 10R groups used only one set of stimuli throughout training; in these groups the 10 training tasks (sets of stimuli) were assigned to Ss in turn. For each S in the 10R groups, the 10 re-pairings of the stimuli and responses were such that no stimulus was ever paired with the same slot more than once.

For the 10-task groups, the 10 training tasks were arranged in 10 completely different orders and the orders were assigned to Ss in turn. For the 2-task and 5-task groups, the training tasks chosen, and the order in which they were practiced, were such that each of the 10 available tasks was used equally often, and about equally often in each position in an order.

Transfer Tests

The first transfer test was given 24 hr. after completion of training, the second 24 hr. later. Each test consisted of 20 trials.[2] Both transfer tasks were used in both tests by splitting each of the 15 main groups of Ss into two subgroups. One set of subgroups was tested with nonsense syllables on the first test, with H figures on the second; for the other set of subgroups the order was reversed.

All Ss worked a 5-day week, so for groups trained 5 days or 10 days, but not for groups trained 2 days, a weekend intervened between end of training and first transfer test.

Subjects and Procedure

The Ss were 600 male and female undergraduates at Northwestern University, paid for their services. There were 40 Ss in each of the 15 main groups, 20 Ss in each of the 30 subgroups.

---

[2] Most of the Ss in Groups 10–10, 10–1, and 10–10R had been given 21 trials on all training and transfer days before it was finally decided to use 20 trials per day as the basic unit. In the course of final matching of all groups about one-third of the Ss in these groups were replaced with Ss given 20 trials a day. Examination of some of the data showed no difference between 20- and 21-trial Ss.

Instructions to S described the nature of the learning task and emphasized making as many correct responses as possible; the latter point was mentioned at beginning of practice each day. Instructions also specified that it was necessary to make one, and only one, response every time a stimulus appeared; thus, there is no independent error measure and the data are reported in terms of correct responses.

Results

Comparability of Groups

Enough Ss were run to permit eventual matching of all 30 subgroups with 20 Ss in each, matched on mean total correct responses on Trials 2–4 of the first training task. (Scores on Trial 1 would be largely chance and some groups received only four trials per task.) The 30 matching means ranged from 6.22 to 6.87; standard errors ranged from .37 to .86. Although it is not known how adequate matching was for groups not given more than four trials on the first task, a check made with some groups given 20 trials on that task showed that matching on Trials 2–4 produced groups that were not significantly different on total score over 20 trials. The correlation, based on 100 Ss, between scores on Trials 2–4 and Trials 2–20 was .46.

Training

Training data will not be presented in detail, but some points are worth noting. In groups trained for several days on one task (e.g., Group 10–1), a few Ss mastered the task (13 correct responses per trial) by the end of the first day, i.e., first 20 trials, and all 40 Ss mastered the task by the end of Day 4. Thus, all Ss in two of the three constant-training groups (Groups 10–1 and 5–1) had thoroughly mastered their one training task before being tested for transfer, but this was not true for Group 2–1. This difference will show up in transfer performance.

Groups trained with several tasks showed improvement in performance on successive tasks, as shown in Figure 1. The six groups depicted in Figure 1 are the three trained with 10 different tasks (left side of Figure 1), and the three trained with 10 re-pairings of the same task (right side), for 2, 5, or 10 days. Each symbol on a solid-line curve in Figure 1 represents mean correct responses per trial over all trials given that gorup on a task (see Table 1). Thus vertical differences among solid-line curves in either side of Figure 1 are of no significance, since the points are based on different numbers of trials. Explanation of the dashed and dotted lines in Figure 1 is given in the legend.

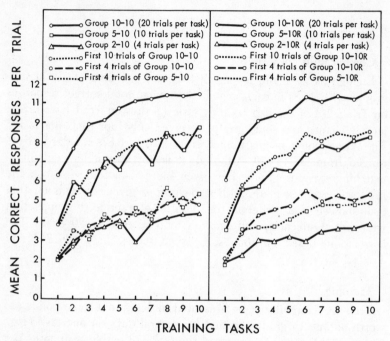

FIGURE 1. Performance during training of the three groups trained with 10 different sets of stimuli, on the left; and of the three groups trained with 10 re-pairing of the same stimuli, on the right.

Figure 1 shows that all groups improved from the first to tenth task. Even the apparently small gain made by Group 2-10R is highly significant; *t* for related measures between the first and tenth tasks was 6.89. It cannot be assumed that re-paired groups learned the same thing as different-task groups; the transfer data will show that they did not.

Comparison of any of the dashed or dotted curves in Figure 1 with the solid-line curve nearest to it gives some indication of whether or not the intertask improvement exhibited in the first 4 (or 10) trials on each task is greater in a group given *more* than 4 (or 10) trials per task than it is in a group given *only* 4 (or 10) trials per task. These comparisons were not analyzed statistically because there are obvious effects due to sequencing of tasks over days, but the curves do suggest that intertask improvement as measured in terms of performance on an early block of trials on each task is greater when each task is practiced beyond the number of trials constituting the block.

Transfer

The data of major interest are performances of groups trained with different tasks and tested on two transfer tasks counterbalanced over two transfer tests. Transfer data for groups trained with re-paired tasks will be analyzed separately. All analyses to be presented are based on total correct responses over all 20 trials given on a transfer task as the score for each S.

First Transfer Test

Since each major group was split into two subgroups, one tested with nonsense syllables, the other with H figures, on the first test, the data were analyzed for three variables: amount of training, number of training tasks, and transfer task. The analysis of variance based on these 24 subgroups (omitting the 6 subgroups trained with re-paired tasks) is summarized in Table 2, where Days and Tasks indicate the two training variables and Transfer indicates transfer task. The test for heterogeneity of variance gave $\chi^2 = 34.22$, which is not significant with 23 df.

Table 2 indicates that none of the interactions between training variables and the transfer-task variable (D × Tr., T × Tr., D × T × Tr.) was significant. It is therefore not necessary to report data for the two transfer tasks separately. In terms of over-all performance there was a significant difference between transfer tasks ($F = 21.01$); performance on H figures was lower.

Both training variables had highly significant effects on transfer, as the Days and Tasks terms in Table 2 show. These effects are shown in the left side of Figure 2, where mean total correct responses is plotted as a function of number of training tasks, with amount of training as the parameter. Since performance on the two transfer tasks is combined, each point is based on 40 Ss. (The

TABLE 2

Comparison of Performance on the First Transfer Test of the Groups Trained with 1, 2, 5, or 10 Different Tasks

Source	df	MS	F
Days (D)	2	34707.08	26.61*
Tasks (T)	3	8875.16	6.81*
Transfer (Tr)	1	27403.53	21.01*
D × T	6	818.34	
D × Tr	2	2651.52	2.03
T × Tr	3	584.52	
D × T × Tr	6	812.44	
Within	456	1304.20	

* $P = .01$.

solid symbols in Figure 2 show performance of re-paired groups, and will be dealt with later.)

Taken together, Table 2 and Figure 2 show that transfer increased both as number of training tasks and as amount of training increased. Even though there is no true control group, it is highly probable that net transfer was positive. First, mean total correct responses on the first *training* task was 125.51 (based on all Ss given at least 20 trials and with all 10 sets of training stimuli represented); no value in Figure 2 is lower than this. Second, the transfer tasks were not easier than the combined training tasks. The best performance in the left side of Figure 2 is by Group 10–10, but even its performance on the easier transfer task (nonsense syllables) was lower than its own mean total score of 207.95 on the last (tenth) training task. Thus, performance on transfer tasks was higher than performance on the combined 10 sets of stimuli making up the first training task very probably because of positive transfer, not merely because the transfer tasks were easier.

Returning to Table 2, it can be seen that the interaction between training variables (D × T) is not significant. This is an important finding and will be discussed later.

Since number of training tasks was significant, the effect on transfer of constant versus varied training can be determined by comparing the mean of the 1-task (constant training) group with means of the 2-, 5-, and 10-task groups. Because no interaction in

Table 2 was significant, groups and subgroups differentiated on other variables were combined to yield means based an 120 Ss each. These means were 143.95, 154.88, 158.85, and 164.23 for the 1-, 2-, 5-, and 10-task groups respectively. Comparison of the 1-task mean with the other three values yielded ts of 2.34, 3.19, and 4.34 re-

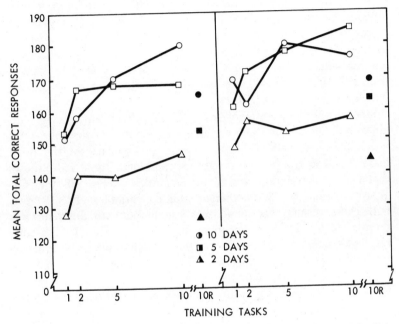

Figure 2. Performance of all groups on the first transfer test, on the left; and on the second test, on the right. Performance on the two transfer tasks is combined within each test.

spectively (standard error of difference obtained from Within Groups term in Table 2). Since all these values are significant at the 2% level or better, it is clear that all degrees of varied training produced better transfer than constant training. There is also some evidence that greater degrees of varied training yielded more transfer than lesser degrees; the 10-task mean is significantly higher than the 2-task mean ($t = 2.00$, $P.05$). Other comparisons were not significant.

Means for groups given different amounts of training were 138.49, 163.58, and 164.37 for the 2-, 5-, and 10-day groups, respectively (all groups attributable to other variables combined, 160 Ss per mean). The 2-day mean is significantly lower than either the 5-day ($t = 6.21$) or 10-day ($t = 6.41$) means; 5- and 10-day values are not significantly different. Not surprisingly, transfer increased, up to a certain point, as a function of amount of training.

The results on the first transfer test of the six subgroups (three amounts of training, two transfer tasks) trained on 10 re-pairings of the same set of stimuli with responses involves the comparison of these Ss with the six constant-training (1-task) subgroups in the analysis summarized in Table 3 (where Tasks indicates the type of training). The test for heterogeneity of variance gave $\chi^2 = 13.50$, which is not significant with 11 df.

Since none of the interactions in Table 3 between training variables and the transfer-task variable was significant, the solid symbols in the left half of Figure 2 show performance of the three main re-paired groups with subgroups combined. Table 3 also shows that Days (of training) and Transfer (task) were significant variables, and that the interaction of training variables ($D \times T$) was not. These results correspond to those found with different-tasks groups (Table 2). But the important term in Table 3 is the one for Tasks, which is not significant; there was no difference in transfer among constant-training and re-paired groups. Thus, practice at associating stimuli with responses, with which re-paired groups had as much experience as did groups trained with 10 different sets

TABLE 3

Comparison of Performance on the First Transfer Test of the Groups Trained with Re-paired Stimuli and the Constant-Training Groups

Source	df	MS	F
Days	2	21210.47	12.34°
Tasks	1	1131.01	
Transfer	1	14492.61	8.43°
$D \times T$	2	1286.02	
$D \times Tr$	2	847.82	
$T \times Tr$	1	495.92	
$D \times T \times Tr$	2	630.61	
Within	228	1718.98	

° $P = .01$.

of stimuli, cannot account for the demonstrated transfer advantage of training with different tasks.

TABLE 4

Analysis of the Effect of Order of Presentation of Transfer Tasks
Over the Two Transfer Tests

Source	df	MS	F
Test	1	25781.90	53.88*
Task	1	83794.75	175.12*
Error	478	478.50	
Order	1	3099.60	1.41
Ss within orders	478	2201.21	

* $P = .01$.

Second Transfer Test

In this test each subgroup was tested with whatever transfer task (nonsense syllables or H figures) it had not practiced on the first test. Since there might be an effect of order of transfer tasks over tests, total correct responses of all four combinations of transfer test and transfer task (obtained by combining all groups attributable to training variables) were compared to permit evaluation of order. The analysis is summarized in Table 4 (groups trained with repaired stimuli are not included).

In Table 4 the term for Order (tested against Ss within orders) is not significant; there is no evidence of an interaction due to order of transfer tasks over tests. Since the term for Task is highly significant (tested against Error), again indicating that over-all performance was lower on H figures than on nonsense syllables, the fact that Order was not significant indicates that there was no differential transfer in going from easy to difficult or from difficult to easy transfer tasks. The significant term for Test (tested against Error) indicates that over-all performance was higher on the second test, presumably due to additional "training" provided by practice on the first test. Most of the gain occurred in groups trained originally with only one task.

Analysis of groups trained with different tasks (performed as illustrated in Table 2) showed that, as on the first test, none of the interactions between the transfer-task variable and training variables was significant. Therefore, performance on the second test, plotted on the right in Figure 2, is shown with subgroups attributable to transfer tasks combined. Over-all difference in performance on the transfer tasks was, as usual, highly significant ($F = 53.74, P = .01$, 1 and 456 df).

Amount of training (Days) was still a highly significant variable on the second test ($F = 17.24$, $P = .01$, 2 and 456 df). But the effect of training with different numbers of tasks was significant only at the 5% level ($F = 3.82$, where 3.83 is needed at the 1% level with 3 and 456 df). This reduced effect of the Tasks variable may be seen, although not too clearly, by comparing steepness of corresponding curves in the left and right sides of Figure 2.

As before, means of the 1-, 2-, 5-, and 10-task groups were compared by t-tests. Both the 5- and 10-task groups were significantly superior to the 1-task group at the 2% level or better (t's of 2.44 and 2.96, respectively), but the 2-task group was not ($t < 1.00$). Thus, on the second test only greater degrees of varied training produced superior transfer to constant training.

Comparison of groups trained with re-paired stimuli with 1-task groups was made by an analysis like that shown in Table 3. As on the first test, the only significant terms were those for Days of training and for Transfer task (both significant at the 1% level); re-paired training produced no better transfer than constant training (F tasks < 1.00). Performance of re-paired groups on the second test is shown by solid symbols on the right side of Figure 2.

Discussion

The major findings were: (a) transfer was a direct function of degree of variation in training; (b) the relation between transfer and degree of variation in training was independent of amount of training.

The finding that transfer increased directly with increases in degree of variation in training supplies the answer to the question with which this study is primarily concerned: varied training produced better transfer than constant training. Furthermore, this result was found for the case where total amount of practice was equal for both constant and varied training. When total practice is equal, there is, of course, much more practice on the one task given in constant training than there is on any one of the tasks used in varied training, but, as the results show, this was not important.

The advantage of varied over constant training was probably not merely the difference between positive transfer and zero transfer, between training and no training. Although there was no control group for transfer per se, there is, as shown earlier, every reason to think that there was net positive transfer from training to transfer tasks. This means that even constant training produced some positive transfer, so the superiority of varied training was measured in terms of even larger amounts of positive transfer.

The second major finding was that there was no interaction between degree of variation in training and amount of training. In other words, the advantage of varied over constant training was not affected by varying total amount of training (as long as total training, whatever its amount, was equal for both varied and constant training conditions). This fact, that there was no interaction between the two training variables, is one more indication that what is important in varied training is variation per se. In short, S learns something from being required to practice with different sets of stimuli, and, as in most learning situations, the most important variable is the number of "trials" (sets of stimuli); the more trials, the more he learns.

In asking what S learns by working with different sets of stimuli it should be noted that we are not dealing with transfer which is based on stimulus or response generalization in the usual sense, or with transfer based on stimulus predifferentiation. Rather, we are concerned with the kind of nonspecific habit or skill that is similar to what has been called learning to learn (McGeoch, 1952) or learning set (Harlow, 1949), and that facilitates transfer among tasks which have overall similarity but which lack easily identifiable dimensions of stimulus or response similarity. But curves of learning to learn and learning set probably overestimate the kind of nonspecific habit with which the studies of Dashiell (1924), Crafts (1927), and the present study were concerned; the progressive improvement such curves show is not entirely due to varied training.

In attempting to infer something about this nonspecific skill, or generalized ability to learn, the data from groups trained with re-paired stimuli are useful. These groups, like groups trained with different sets of stimuli, had to start from scratch on every new "task" (re-pairing), and also showed considerable improvement from their first to their tenth re-pairing. Yet, unlike different-task Ss they showed no better transfer than Ss given constant training. (It should be noted that the transfer tasks involved new stimuli, and so may not be the most appropriate tasks for testing re-paired groups.) Thus, the generalized learning skill developed by Ss trained with different sets of stimuli is not due to response differentiation or other factors on the response side, nor to experience at associating stimuli and responses. All of these factors should be the same from training with either different stimuli or re-paired stimuli. The skill is also not due to such factors as getting used to the situation, reduction of tension, etc., since these should be the same for any kind of training, including constant training, when total practice, and therefore total time in the situation, is the same. It seems clear that the generalized skill that facilitated transfer performance in the present study was developed only from experience with different sets of stimuli.

Attempts to specify the basis of a skill which is developed from experience with stimuli have been made by other writers. Crafts' (1927) suggestion was that varied training compelled the development of habits of looking, searching, exploring, as habits antecedent to the final response. Kurtz (1955) believed that S develops "observing responses." Reid (1953) suggested a "response of discriminating." Eckstrand and Wickens (1954) suggested that Ss develop a "perceptual set," that during varied training S becomes more sensitive to relevant than to irrelevant dimensions among stimuli.

The writer's view is very similar to those cited. Varied training seems to force S to pay close attention to every stimulus in every set. In time this response of concentrated attention may become habitual; S may learn, as a general, transferable principle, that it is of value to look carefully at each stimulus presented, not only to its obvious characteristics, but also to any minor details. If S does this, he should be able to discriminate easily among the stimuli within a list and between different lists, thus minimizing both intralist and interlist interference. (Riopelle, 1953, has already shown that suppression of intertask interference aids the development of learning sets.) In short, it is hypothesized that training with a variety of stimuli forces S to concentrate carefully on every stimulus, making use of all cues the stimulus provides, and that as a result stimuli soon became easily discriminable and enter more readily into S–R associations.

From this hypothesis it would be predicted that amount (not necessarily rate) both of learning to learn in the simple sense of intertask improvement, and of the generalized ability to learn, should vary directly with degree of intralist, and perhaps interlist, similarity, and inversely with meaningfulness of stimuli. Evidence bearing on these predictions is not at present available.

Summary

Transfer among perceptual-motor paired-associates tasks was studied as a function of two variables: degree of variation in training, which was defined in terms of the number of different sets of training stimuli, and amount of training. Different groups of Ss were trained with 1, 2, 5, or 10 tasks (different sets of stimuli) for 2, 5, or 10 days (20 trials per day). Some other groups were trained for 2, 5, or 10 days with 10 different re-pairings of the responses with a single set of stimuli. Following training, all Ss were tested for transfer to two new sets of stimuli.

The results were:

1. Among groups trained with different sets of stimuli, transfer increased as a direct function of degree of variation in training. In general, when total amount of training was equal, all degrees of varied training (2, 5, or 10 tasks) produced better transfer than constant training (1 task).

2. There was no interaction between degree of variation in training and amount of training; although transfer increased, up to a limit, as total training increased, the transfer superiority of varied over constant training was not significantly affected by changes in amount of training.

3. Groups trained by re-pairing the same stimuli with the responses exhibited, as did groups trained with different sets of stimuli, considerable intertask improvement during training, but showed no better transfer than constant training.

It was suggested that these results may be best interpreted in terms of observational or perceptual processes.

[6]
Transfer in Perceptual Learning Following Stimulus Predifferentiation [1]

HENRY C. ELLIS and DOUGLAS G. MULLER

Two experiments on stimulus predifferentiation were conducted to test the acquired distinctiveness of cues and differentiation hypotheses of perceptual learning. In the first, 240 Ss were given a recognition test following stimulus predifferentiation training. Observation training yielded superior recognition of 6-point shapes and distinctiveness pretraining yielded superior recognition of 24-point shapes. The former result was consistent with differentiation theory and the latter with acquired distinctiveness. In the second, 30 Ss received stimulus predifferentiation training followed by a discriminative transfer task. Distinctiveness pretraining yielded greater positive transfer than observation, a result consistent with acquired distinctiveness of cues.

The hypothesis of acquired distinctiveness of cues (Goss, 1955, Miller and Dollard, 1941) states that attaching a response such as a verbal label to a stimulus tends to increase the distinctiveness of that stimulus as a result of the addition of response-produced cues. Presumably, different verbal labels attached to similar stimuli will increase the distinctiveness of the stimuli, whereas similar or identical verbal labels attached to different stimuli will reduce the distinctiveness of the stimuli. An alternative conception of the perceptual learning process has been proposed by Gibson and Gibson (1955), that of differentiation, which contends that organisms learn to distinguish various components which are inherent in the stimulus; perceptual learning consists of responding to various

---

[1] The research was supported by National Science Foundation Grant G-23427.

Thanks are due to James M. Vanderplas for his review of the manuscript, and to Thomas L. Bennett and Dieter Jahns who assisted in the conduct of the study.

SOURCE: H. C. Ellis and D. G. Muller, "Transfer in Perceptual Learning Following Stimulus Predifferentiation," *The Journal of Experimental Psychology*, 1964, 68, 388–395. Reprinted by permission of the American Psychological Association.

stimuli not previously responded to rather than adding response-produced cues to stimuli. As Vanderplas (1963) has noted, the Miller-Dollard view implies a dependence on the nature of the labeling response whereas the Gibson view implies no such dependence. Several experiments designed to test deductions from the distinctiveness of cues hypothesis have failed to confirm it. Similarly, the differentiation hypothesis has not found unequivocal support.

Studies of transfer of predifferentiation training (e.g., Goss and Greenfeld, 1958) have frequently indicated that learning verbal labels to stimuli facilitates performance in some subsequent task when that task requires making new differential responses to the same stimuli. In contrast, experiments which have employed more direct tests of improvement in recognition or discrimination following practice in labeling have generally yielded negative results (Arnoult, 1953; Campbell and Freeman, 1955; Ellis, Bessemer, Devine, and Trafton, 1962; Robinson, 1955), in that no facilitation in these tasks has occurred as a result of distinctiveness labeling practice per se.

Conceivably, whether or not verbal labeling of stimuli improves subsequent discriminative behavior over that improvement associated with observation practice may depend upon the nature of the criterion task employed. In short, practice in verbal labeling of stimuli may be superior to observation practice when the criterion task requires new differential responses to be made to the stimuli. On the other hand, when the task is one of recognition or discrimination or more generally, one which does *not* require making new differential responses to the stimuli, labeling per se may not result in improvement. A similar view has been expressed by Vanderplas (1963).

Since the results of both types of experiments have been employed to support either the hypothesis of acquired distinctiveness or that of differentiation, it seemed desirable to conduct an experiment in which the effect of practice in labeling stimuli would be determined on both discriminative motor transfer and recognition tasks. By controlling the features of the predifferentiation task (e.g., nature of the stimuli, response labels, amount and type of practice) it is possible to determine if the divergencies cited above are dependent upon the criterion task itself.

It is also possible, however, that failure to obtain improvement in recognition following verbal labeling practice is due to other than task variables. For example, Arnoult (1956) found that for very short periods of practice, Ss given labeling practice were superior to those given observation practice in a subsequent test of shape recognition. Vanderplas and Garvin (1959) have shown that shape complexity and association value of random shapes interact with practice in their effect on shape recognition. In view of these alternatives, it was considered desirable to conduct an initial factorial experiment to determine the independent and interactive effects of shape complexity, amount of practice, and type of predifferentiation training on shape recognition. Shape complexity and amount of practice were selected as variables because of their known interactive effect on shape recognition, and three types of training were employed to test the hypotheses of acquired distinctiveness, equivalence, and differentiation. The second experiment was designed to determine the effects of task variables, i.e., to compare the effects of predifferentiation on recognition vs. a motor-switching task.

Experiment I

Method

EXPERIMENTAL DESIGN.   Ten Ss were assigned at random to each of 24 conditions of the experiment. Two levels of stimulus complexity (6- or 24-point random shapes), three types of predifferentiation training (distinctiveness, observation, or equivalence practice), and four levels of practice (2, 4, 8, or 16 trials) were employed. A total of 240 volunteer university students served as Ss.

The experiment was conducted in two parts: In the first part (predifferentiation training) Ss either learned to associate a meaningful response to each of a set of eight random shapes or they were given practice in observing and discriminating among the same set of shapes. Following predifferentiation training, Ss were given a multiple shape recognition test in which they attempted to select from a group of shapes those shapes experienced during predifferentiation training.

STIMULUS SHAPES AND APPARATUS.   A list of eight random shapes was selected from both the 6-point shapes and the 24-point shapes scaled by Vanderplas and Garvin (1959). Table 1 shows the list of shapes employed and their corresponding labels for the distinctiveness and equivalence training groups. The shapes were photographed on 35-mm. filmstrip and presented with a conventional projector (SVE Instructor). Stimulus presentation was controlled by a Foringer self-recycling timer.

TABLE 1

List of Vanderplas and Garvin Shapes and Corresponding Labels
for the Distinctiveness and Equivalence Groups

6-Point Shape No.	Label		24-Point Shape No.	Label	
	Distinct- iveness	Equiva- lence		Distinct- iveness	Equiva- lence
11	Mountain	Wide	10	Tree	Narrow
12	Fish	Narrow	11	Mountain	Wide
13	Rocket	Narrow	12	Bird	Narrow
14	House	Wide	13	Nun	Narrow
15	Boat	Wide	14	Crab	Wide
17	Mouth	Narrow	15	Horseman	Wide
18	Arrow	Narrow	16	Dragon	Narrow
20	Bird	Wide	17	Spider	Wide

PREDIFFERENTIATION TRAINING. The Ss received one of three types of predifferentiation training: distinctiveness, equivalence, or observation practice. The Ss given distinctiveness practice were required to learn relevant meaningful labels to each of eight random shapes. The labels were obtained from a preliminary scaling study in which 30 Ss were shown the shapes and asked to state "what they looked like." The most frequent response given to a particular shape (modal label) was selected for this experiment; modal labels were employed since it was assumed that they would tend to maximize the distinctiveness of the stimuli.

Similarly, Ss given equivalence practice were given an equal number of predifferentiation training trials; the label "wide" was learned for four shapes and the label "narrow" was learned for the remaining four shapes. This procedure was analogous to that of Robinson (1955) and Ellis, Bessemer, Devine, and Trafton (1962) in defining equivalence practice.

The Ss given observation practice were given the same number of pre-differentiation trials except that they were given no labels to attach to the stimuli and were instructed only to inspect the shapes and differentiate among them. For the labeling groups (distinctiveness and equivalence) each stimulus shape was exposed for a 4-sec. period consisting of a 2-sec. anticipation interval and a 2-sec. simultaneous presentation with the response label. Labels were pronounced by S; correct anticipations and errors were recorded. The observation group observed the shapes for the same time interval as did the labeling groups. All Ss were tested individually.

RECOGNITION TEST. Following predifferentiation training, all Ss were immediately given a recognition test which consisted of presenting S with

16 cards, each containing a set of five shapes mounted in a row. Eight of the cards contained a prototype, a shape learned or observed during pre-differentiation, and the remaining four shapes on each card were variations of the prototype. On the remaining eight cards all five shapes were variations of the prototype. Variations were constructed according to a method described by Vanderplas and Garvin (1959). The Ss were instructed to point to a shape if they thought it was one which they learned or observed during predifferentiation training; if they thought that none of the shapes were ones they experienced initially, they were instructed to say "none." The Ss were given no longer than 30 sec. for each card. Five types of responses were recorded: SOP, correct selection of a prototype shape; SOV, incorrect selection of a variation when a prototype was present; IR, incorrect rejection of shapes when one of them was a prototype; SIV, incorrect selection of variation when all shapes were variations; and CR, correct rejection of all shapes when all were variations.

Results

ORIGINAL LEARNING. Table 2 shows the results of original learning on the predifferentiation task and indicates that 16 practice trials were adequate to ensure near mastery of the paired-associate task for both the distinctiveness and equivalence training groups. The mean number of correct anticipations ranged from a low of 2.5 after 2 trials to a high of 7.9 after 16 trials. The table also shows an initial difference in rate of learning favoring the equivalence groups, which reflects the fact that this group was required to learn only two response labels, as opposed to the eight labels required of the distinctiveness group. No test of the significance of this trend was made, however, since the data of primary interest were the scores on the recognition test.

TABLE 2

Mean Correct Anticipations during Predifferentiation Training for Labeling Groups

Type of Training	Shape Complexity	Trials			
		2	4	8	16
Distinctiveness	6-point	2.5	5.5	6.9	7.4
	24-point	2.8	4.7	6.5	7.7
Equivalence	6-point	5.7	6.3	7.6	7.9
	24-point	4.4	5.5	6.7	6.2

RECOGNITION PERFORMANCE. The basic data obtained in the recognition test, the number of correct recognitions (SOP responses), are shown in Table 3. The table shows that the observation group tended to make more correct recognitions of simple shapes than did either group receiving labeling practice. A clear trend of increased recognition with increased practice is evident and the groups retained their same relative ranks with increase in practice.

Table 3 shows that with *complex* shapes, the distinctiveness group makes more correct recognitions than the observation groups after 2, 4, or 8 practice trials. In short, if labels are attached to stimuli of high complexity, recognition is superior to that provided by observation practice; if labels are attached to stimuli of low complexity, recognition is poorer than that provided by observation practice. This finding suggests an interaction between the effects of shape complexity and type of training, an interpretation which is supported by the significant $C \times T$ interaction (see Table 4: $F = 3.95$). Both the effects of amount of practice and type of practice on prototype recognition were reliable.

Table 3 shows the results of the remaining four recognition tests. The mean number of selection of variations when the prototype was present (SOV), incorrect rejections (IR), selection of variations when all shapes were variations (SIV), and correct rejections (CR) are shown. Separate analyses of variance were performed for each response type and the results are shown in Table 4.[2]

From Table 3 it may be seen that practice leads to a reduction of IR responses for all types of predifferentiation training and a reduction of SIV responses for the distinctiveness and observation groups. Similarly, practice leads to an increase of CR responses for the distinctiveness and observation groups. No systematic changes occur in SIV or CR responses with increasing amounts of equivalence training. The analyses of variance resulted in a significant variance for practice effects for all response types (Table 4). Table 3 also indicates that the distinctiveness and observation groups tend to make fewer SOV responses to either 6- or 24-point shapes; this finding is supported by the significant F for type of training: (see Table 4: $F = 9.07$).

[2] No analysis of variance on the CR responses is reported. The CR responses are determined by the number of SIV responses and both must sum to eight. Since CR responses are fixed, an analysis of variance on CR responses yields the same results as an analysis of variance on SIV responses.

TABLE 3

**Mean Number of Correct Responses (SOP), Incorrect Selections When
Prototype Was Present (SOV), Incorrect Rejections (IR), Incorrect
Selections When All Shapes Were Variations (SIV), and Correct
Rejections (CR) for Each Condition of the Experiment**

Type of Training	Practice Trials	Response Types				
		SOP	SOV	IR	SIV	CR
6-Point Shapes						
Distinctiveness	2	2.8	2.2	3.0	4.3	3.7
	4	3.5	2.7	1.8	3.6	4.4
	8	4.9	1.3	1.8	3.3	4.7
	16	5.7	0.9	1.4	2.3	5.7
Observation	2	3.3	2.1	2.6	4.1	3.9
	4	3.9	2.0	2.1	3.1	4.9
	8	5.8	1.0	1.2	2.9	5.1
	16	6.1	1.0	0.9	2.3	5.7
Equivalence	2	1.9	3.4	2.7	4.1	3.9
	4	2.1	3.0	2.9	4.0	4.0
	8	3.7	2.1	2.2	3.4	4.6
	16	4.0	2.4	1.6	4.5	3.5
24-Point Shapes						
Distinctiveness	2	2.6	2.3	3.1	4.1	3.9
	4	4.0	1.1	2.9	2.7	5.3
	8	4.7	0.9	2.4	1.9	6.1
	16	6.3	0.5	1.2	1.9	6.1
Observation	2	2.0	2.4	3.6	3.2	4.8
	4	3.1	1.9	3.0	2.7	5.3
	8	3.5	2.5	2.0	3.8	4.2
	16	6.7	0.5	0.8	1.5	6.5
Equivalence	2	2.5	2.7	2.8	3.6	4.4
	4	2.1	3.1	2.8	3.6	4.4
	8	3.2	2.3	2.5	3.2	4.8
	16	5.2	1.2	1.6	3.3	4.7

TABLE 4

Analysis of Variance of Scores on Recognition Test for Each
Response Type

| Source | df | Response Type | | | |
| | | SOP | SOV | IR | SIV |
		F	F	F	F
Complexity (C)	1	.55	1.12	4.22 *	5.53 *
Practice (P)	3	47.23 ‡	9.32 ‡	16.71 ‡	5.37 †
Type of training (T)	2	16.10 ‡	9.07 ‡	1.31	4.64 †
C × P	3	3.34 *	1.45	.90	.26
C × T	2	3.95 *	1.60	.85	.30
P × T	6	.89	.26	.90	2.08
C × P × T	6	.55	.00	.32	.81
Error (MS)	216	(2.46)	(2.69)	(1.99)	(3.09)

* $p < .05$.
† $p < .01$.
‡ $p < .001$.

Experiment II

The purpose of Experiment II was to determine if positive transfer to an instrumental motor task would occur following practice in labeling shapes under conditions in which the same labeling practice, as compared with observation practice, did *not* lead to superior recognition.

Method

EXPERIMENTAL DESIGN. Fifteen Ss were assigned at random to each of the two conditions of the experiment. One group received distinctiveness training and the other received observation training, identical to that given in Experiment I. Following predifferentiation training, Ss were given a criterion task which required them to learn to press a switch for each of the eight shapes they had labeled or observed.

CONDITIONS OF THE EXPERIMENT. The Ss labeled or observed only the 6-point shapes employed in Experiment I. These shapes were used because the distinctiveness labeling group was inferior to the observation group in the recognition of 6-point shapes (see Table 3). Since these findings were typical of those of other *Es*, they were used for purposes of comparison with findings with the motor transfer task. The same apparatus, procedure, labels, etc., employed in the predifferentiation part of

Experiment I were used in the predifferentiation part of Experiment II. The Ss were given 16 practice trials.

INSTRUMENTAL TRANSFER TASK. Following predifferentiation training, all Ss were immediately given a transfer task which required them to learn to press one of eight switches located on a response panel for each of the eight shapes they had previously experienced. Each stimulus shape was exposed for 2 sec. and S was instructed to press the switch as rapidly as he could. All Ss received 15 trial blocks of training; a block consisted of a single presentation of each of eight shapes which were presented in random order. The Ss were given confirmation of their correct responses by the appearance of a green light; an incorrect response was followed by no signal. Both correct responses and latency, the time between presentation of the shape and S's response, were recorded.

Results

PERFORMANCE ON THE MOTOR TRANSFER TASK. Inspection of Figure 1 reveals that Ss given distinctiveness practice in labeling 6-point

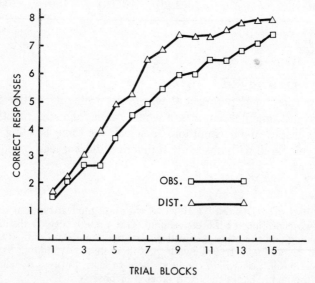

FIGURE 1. Mean number of correct motor-switching responses to 6-point shapes following predifferentiation training.

shapes are superior in acquisition of a motor-switching task compared with Ss given practice in observing the shapes. After Trial 3 the distinctiveness group was clearly superior and retained its superiority throughout the remaining trials. An analysis of variance applied to the transfer data indicated that the difference between the two groups was reliable ($F = 6.53; p < .05$).

LATENCY. Examination of the latency data revealed that Ss given distinctiveness practice showed a consistent overall tendency to respond faster than did Ss given observation practice. An analysis of variance applied to the latency data, however, did not reveal a significant difference between the two groups.

DISCUSSION

The findings of the recognition experiment indicate that although shape complexity itself was not a significant variable in affecting the number of correct recognitions, it did interact with type of predifferentiation training. Specifically, the results indicated that attaching distinctive verbal labels to complex shapes facilitated their subsequent recognition whereas distinctiveness labeling practice with simple shapes did not facilitate their subsequent recognition, when compared with control groups given practice in observing and discriminating among the shapes. The results with complex shapes lend some support to the hypothesis of acquired distinctiveness of cues based upon distinctive response-produced cues being added to the stimuli. In contrast, the results with simple shapes are at least consistent with differentiation theory.

The problem remains as to how to explain the interactive effects of shape complexity and type of training on shape recognition. A tentative explanation is given below based upon some assumptions about labeling practice and stimulus familiarity. Let us assume that when S learns to attach a label to a simple shape, there are relatively few cues which require differentiation. Therefore, S does not have to expend great effort in scanning the shape and differentiating cues. In addition, if we assume that simple shapes are more familiar than complex shapes, then S will be able to relate more readily the simple shape to some available concept. Thus, the effect of labeling practice on the recognition of simple shapes, as compared with observation practice, would be minimal since the simple shapes are already relatively distinctive and familiar. On the other hand, complex shapes have many more aspects to which S must attend, and are less readily or easily related to some concept. The effect of a label then, if relevant, is to provide a concept to which the shape may be related. In the absence of any immediate labels, as is the case with observation practice, S would be required to select concepts to which the shape could be related. This would require more effort and time on the part of Ss given observation practice and would explain why Ss given observation practice would be inferior in tasks of complex shape recognition as compared with Ss given labeling practice. Finally, this approach would predict that after relatively extensive practice, Ss given observation practice with complex shapes would do as well in recognition tests as Ss given labeling practice because they would have had sufficient opportunity to acquire a label to attach to the shape. This latter assumption is consistent with the fact that although labeling practice facilitated the recognition of complex shapes after 2, 4, and 8 trials, the labeling practice group performed approximately the same as the observation practice group after 16 trials.

The results of equivalence practice are consistent for both simple and complex shapes. In both instances, Ss who received equivalence pretraining made fewer correct recognitions than either the distinctiveness or observation groups. These findings appear consistent with the hypothesis of acquired equivalence of cues and are consistent with those obtained in a study of tactual recognition (Ellis, Bessemer, Devine, and Trafton, 1962).

The results of the second experiment reveal that practice in giving stimuli distinctive verbal labels leads to greater positive transfer in a discriminative motor task than does observation of the stimuli alone. This finding can be interpreted as being consistent with the hypothesis of acquired distinctiveness of cues; however, the fact that the discriminability of the stimuli was not similarly enhanced, as measured by a recognition test, raises some doubt about this interpretation. It seems equally reasonable to suggest that enhanced positive transfer to an instrumental task could occur not only as a result of increased distinctiveness of the stimuli, but also as a result of increased availability of motor and other responses. In other words, learning to attach verbal responses to stimuli may facilitate the attachment of other types of responses to these stimuli, but may *not* necessarily produce increased distinctiveness of the stimuli. In order to determine if positive transfer to an instrumental motor task following labeling practice is to be interpreted as due to increased distinctiveness of the stimuli, or to increased availability of responses, or both, it is necessary to design an experiment in which either stimulus distinctiveness or response availability is controlled.

The findings of the present experiment indicate only that an explanation of the positive transfer findings in terms of a response availability hypothesis is as reasonable as a distinctiveness of cues hypothesis.

[7]
Effects of Group Experience on Individual Problem Solving

BRYCE B. HUDGINS

A number of investigators (Gurnee, 1937, Klugman, 1944, Perlmutter and de Montmollin, 1952, Taylor and Faust, 1952) have examined the relative effectiveness of problem solving by groups and by individuals. In general, they have found that groups furnish more correct solutions to problems than comparable subjects do working as individuals. The present inquiry continues in this tradition, and attempts to extend knowledge in the area by providing experimental answers to two questions related to the problem solving behavior of elementary school children. First, do children working together in groups learn techniques of problem solving which they can apply later in similar situations, and, secondly, does interaction, as herein defined, contribute to the superiority of group problem solving? A casual inspection of elementary school principles of teaching texts would suggest that this transfer and the conditions under which it occurs are demonstrated facts rather than unanswered problems.

Answers to these questions hinged on the assumption that groups of children would be more successful in solving problems than their counterparts working individually. This result had been so well

SOURCE: B. B. Hudgins, "Effects of Group Experience on Individual Problem Solving," *The Journal of Educational Psychology*, 1960, Vol. **51**, No. 1, pp. 37–42. Reprinted by permission of B. B. Hudgins and the American Psychological Association.

demonstrated in the past that there seemed little reason to doubt that it could be replicated in a school situation.

Additional significance of the study lies in the use of "natural groups." The use of *ad hoc* groups has been criticized in a survey of investigations of group and individual performance.

A common and dangerous practice is to generalize the principles valid for *ad hoc* groups to traditioned groups. The *ad hoc* group is treated as a microscopic model of the traditioned group. This might be true, but has not been experimentally validated. It is equally possible that *ad hoc* and traditioned groups behave in accordance with their individual principles (Lorge, Fox, Davitz, and Brenner, 1958).

The groups used in this study were *ad hoc* in the sense that they were organized for purposes of the investigation. It seems to the writer that what constitutes a traditioned group depends upon the context in which the group is found. It can be argued that groups which operate for three consecutive days, as in the present study, approximate traditioned groups as they exist in the classroom. The analogy here is between the experimental groups and others which are formed for a specific activity within the classroom.

HYPOTHESES AND RATIONALE

Three hypotheses were formulated to provide a basis for answering the questions asked above:

1. The first hypothesis was that problem solving experience in a group improves individual ability more than does individual experience.

It was hypothesized that when subjects (Ss) who had worked on arithmetic problem as members of a group were tested individually, their mean score would be significantly higher than the mean of Ss who had worked individually throughout the experiment. This answers the first question above, concerning the carry-over from the group situation to a subsequent individual one.

2. The second hypothesis was that individual ability to solve arithmetic problems improves as a result of specifying the steps involved in arriving at solution.

Specification consisted of providing written answers to a series of questions which were intended to lead Ss toward problem solution. There were four questions which specification subjects had to answer in connection with the solution of each problem:

1. What are you asked to find?
2. What information are you given that will help you find the answer?
3. What do you have to do to find the answer?
4. What is the answer?

It was predicted that the mean score of Ss who had worked under the condition of specification would be significantly higher than the mean of Ss who had not used specification.

Underlying this hypothesis was the reasoning that disagreement among group members about a solution initiates a review process during which the attention of individual members is directed to the various critical steps in problem solution. The group's contribution to successful problem solving, then, lies in "instructing" the participants in proper problem solving procedure. If this is true, the student working alone who is required to specify the steps by which progress is made toward problem solution will improve much as if he were exposed to the influence of the group. Thus, the group influence may be an artifact, seemingly important, but only because it invokes a process which one ordinarily would not use, but would be capable of using, in isolation.

3. A final hypothesis was that the improvement of problem solving ability as a result of group experience stems from the relevancy of intragroup communication to the processes involved in problem solution.

That is, students tested individually following a period of time in which they had worked as members of a group using specification would solve significantly more problems than subjects who worked initially in nonspecification groups. By systematizing the "instruction" process in the group situation, presumably even greater gains in individual problem solving success will be realized.

In short, is there carry-over in the form of higher individual performance as a consequence of the group experience, and does a structuring of problem solving procedures account for a portion of the variation in pupil performance?

METHOD

Sample

The Ss of the investigation were 128 fifth-grade students selected in equal numbers from each of four public schools in the city of St. Louis.

Controls

A measure of each S's general mental ability and arithmetic problem solving ability was made immediately prior to the experiment. The general mental ability test used was the California Test of Mental Maturity, Short Form. Arithmetic ability was measured by the California Arithmetic Test, Elementary, Grades 4-5-6, Form W.

The 32 Ss in each classroom were matched by fours on the basis of their general ability and arithmetic test scores, and assigned to one of four experimental groups. The assignment of the 8 Ss in each group to an experimental condition was done by reference to a table of random numbers. Following the final assignment there was no significant difference in either general mental ability or arithmetic ability among the groups prior to the experiment.

During the experiment, the groups from two of the classes were taken to a room other than their regular classroom. In the other two classes, Ss working individually were taken to another room, while the groups remained in their homeroom. This was done in order that the novelty of a new working environment would not exercise a systematic influence on any one of the experimental conditions.

Tasks

The arithmetic problems from Forms J, K, L, and M of the Stanford Achievement Test, Intermediate, were used as experimental materials. The following are 2 problems out of the total 120 which Ss were asked to solve.

Bill jumped 13 feet, 5 inches on Tuesday. On Thursday he jumped 11 feet, 9 inches. How much farther did he jump on Tuesday than on Thursday?

The butcher says to cook a turkey 20 minutes for each pound. At what hour should a 15 pound turkey be started in order to be done at twelve o'clock noon?

Procedures, Phase 1

The first phase consisted of three consecutive days of problem solving using Forms J, K, and L of the Stanford. The 128 pupils worked as follows: Thirty-two pupils (called A Ss) worked in subgroups of four students. Each subgroup had to agree on a single answer to each question in the specifications.

Another 32 pupils (B Ss) also worked in four member groups. Within each group, members were free to develop their own methods for solving the problems. The only restriction imposed upon them was that the group must arrive at one answer to each problem.

Half of the 64 pupils working individually (C Ss) used the method of specification. The other half (D Ss) were simply instructed to solve the problems and to record each solution in the appropriate space on the problem sheets.

Procedures, Phase 2

This portion of the experiment consisted of the 128 students solving individually the 30 problems in Form M of the Stanford. To ascertain the possible effects of differential retention, all the Ss from one classroom (i.e., one-fourth of the total sample) were tested on each of the following days after the completion of Phase 1—the first, second, fifth, and twelfth day. In this way, one-fourth of the A, B, C, and D Ss were tested on each day of Phase 2.

Results

Phase 1

Throughout the three days of Phase 1, Ss who worked in groups made higher scores than Ss working individually. On the first day the mean score of Ss working in groups (A and B) was 18.82; that for Ss working individually (C and D) was 12.80. The mean score for individuals rose on the second day to 13.13, while the groups' mean was only 17.69. On the final day, group Ss had a mean of 20.81 correct responses as compared with 14.91 for individuals. The difference for each of the three days of Phase 1 was significant beyond the .01 level. If these differences had not occurred, there would have been no basis for testing the hypotheses in Phase 2. Any reason for expecting that transfer might result from the group experience, or that specification might be useful as an explanatory concept, would have been lacking. It is for these reasons that Phase 1, which simply demonstrated an already well established finding, was an essential part of the experiment. It confirmed the condition upon which the appropriateness of tests of the three hypotheses depended.

The mean of the Ss using specification (Conditions A and C) was

13.88 for the first day. The mean of the B and D Ss (conditions of nonspecification) for the same day was 17.74. This difference was significant beyond the .05 level. On the second and third days of the first phase, there was no significant difference between the specification and nonspecification conditions. However, the B Ss (who worked in groups without specification) achieved higher scores during Phase 1 than Ss working under any of the other three experimental conditions.

TABLE 1

Mean Score on Arithmetic Problems for Each Phase 1 Experimental Condition and Each Day of Phase 2

Phase 1 Experimental Condition	Day on which Phase 2 Was Administered				
	1 (N = 32)	2 (N = 32)	5 (N = 32)	12 (N = 32)	Mean
A: Groups with specification	15.25	17.25	10.75	15.25	14.63
B: Groups without specification	17.38	19.38	14.25	13.75	16.19
C: Individuals with specification	16.25	14.63	16.38	13.25	15.13
D: Individuals without specification	19.13	15.75	12.88	12.75	15.13
Mean	17.00	16.75	13.57	13.75	15.27

Phase 2

Table 1 gives the mean scores for Phase 2 of Ss who had worked under each of the four experimental conditions, and the mean of each class which received Phase 2 on a given day, respectively. As revealed by Table 2, none of the differences among Ss in Phase 2 was significant.

These findings indicated that, although groups of students working cooperatively solve more problems than comparable students working alone, there is no significant improvement in the problem solving performance of the former Ss because of this group experience. Consequently, the first hypothesis was rejected. Nor were the other two hypotheses supported; that is, practice in specifying the

TABLE 2

Summary Table of Analysis of Variance of Phase 2 Scores

Source	df	Mean Square	F	p
X: Groups versus individuals	1	2.53	.09	$> .05$
Y: Specification versus nonspecification	1	19.53	.70	$> .05$
Z: Retention groups	3	111.03	3.99	$> .05$
XY: Interaction	1	19.54	.70	$> .05$
XZ: Interaction	3	48.28	1.73	$> .05$
YZ: Interaction	3	19.87	.71	$> .05$
XYZ: Interaction	3	27.84	.89	$> .05$
Within	112	31.31		
Total	127			

steps used in solving a problem did not improve performance any more than in the case where such specification was not made. This was true whether specification was used by individuals or by small groups.

DISCUSSION

One problem undertaken by this investigation was an attempt to offer a valid explanation of the superiority of the group over individual problem solving activity. It was hypothesized that this superiority must somehow grow out of the interaction among members working together in the group.

The results of the experiment are clearly opposed to the acceptance of such an hypothesis. However, it must be remembered that the interaction used in this investigation was of a particular type which has been designated specification. It cannot be said with certainty that interaction per se does not affect the quality of the group product. It is possible that, in another form, interaction may contribute to the group superiority.

For example, two interaction patterns were observed in the nonspecification groups during Phase 1. In some of the groups there was a tendency for one S to determine the answer and to communicate it to the other group members. If this person had status as a class leader, his solutions were accepted unquestioningly by the other group members. If he did not have such status, the correctness of his solutions had to be demonstrated before they were accepted.

The second pattern was a more cooperative one which approximated the pattern of the specification groups except for one difference. In these groups each S read the problem and solved it independently. The answers were then compared. If all the answers were identical, the solution was accepted; but if there was disagreement, one person usually took the initiative to demonstrate the appropriateness of the solution to the deviant member or members.

A point of interest arose from the way in which these solutions were determined. Suppose the problem under consideration to be the following: "Our team scored 16 points in the first game, 6 points in the second, and 14 in the third. How many points did we score in all three games?" If there was disagreement about the answer, one person would try to remove the confusion. The usual form of this was to say, "Sixteen and six are twenty-two and fourteen are thirty-six." Such unarguable logic was usually enough to convince the deviant member. On rare occasions the individual said, "You have to add to solve this problem." This remark was followed by the computation.

At no time was there any evidence of attention being given to the first two questions assigned to the specification groups. Such specification as occurred was related to the questions of deciding upon a process appropriate for the solution, and of finding the answer itself. No student was observed justifying his reason for selecting a particular process. Obviously when an incorrect process was selected and agreed upon, the resulting wrong answer tended to receive enthusiastic if misguided support.

Why did the group Ss fail to make higher scores than the C and D Ss on the final test? The answer to this question seems to lie in understanding how the Phase 1 tasks were approached by the members of both kinds of groups. Specification, which was used by half of the groups in Phase 1, provides a systematic means of attacking arithmetic problems. It was assumed that the correct answer to a problem would be found if Ss followed the prescribed steps and if the appropriate computational skills were known and could be used by them. It was also assumed that Ss who used specification in Phase 1 would see the applicability of the method when they were later confronted by similar problems, i.e., in Phase 2. The Phase 2 scores of "groups with specification" Ss lead to the conclusion that there was no transfer from the group to the individual situation of the *steps* which were used in the training period.

As for members of nonspecification groups, it is probable that little if any problem solving skill was acquired in the training period. Their attention seems to have been focused upon accomplishing the task at hand with little regard for developing skills which would be useful in subsequent cases.

The importance for transfer of generalized experience has been demonstrated by Judd (1908) and by Hendrickson and Schroeder (1941). Furthermore, Kingsley and Garry (1957, p. 508) point out "that the mere knowledge of the principle will not insure transfer of training to new situations. Its general applicability must be realized, and the learner must be able to see the possibility of its application to the new situation."

This is a significant point for the present discussion. Prior to the experiment, Ss were told the nature of the condition under which they would work. They were also informed that at a later time they would be asked to solve additional problems by themselves. Little emphasis was placed upon this statement, and no attempt was made to instruct specification Ss that the task given them was one which might help them later in solving problems.

Despite the failure of specification to account for the superiority of groups over individuals, it is still possible, as indicated above, that interaction is related to this superiority. The most reasonable hypothesis at this point appears to be that the problem solving superiority of small groups depends upon the efforts of the most able member of the group to communicate his knowledge to others, and upon the degree to which he achieves acceptance of his solutions. If this hypothesis proves tenable, transfer from the group to the individual situation would not be expected to occur.

SUMMARY

This study inquired (*a*) whether specification (citing the steps leading to solution) is related to the problem solving superiority of small groups over individuals and (*b*) whether individual problem solving ability improves as a result of group experience.

Subjects were 128 fifth-grade girls and boys. The first phase of the study lasted three days during which subjects worked on sets of arithmetic problems under an experimental condition. Half worked as group members; half as individuals. Group members solved significantly more problems than subjects who worked alone.

In Phase 2, all subjects worked individually. No differences were found among subjects' scores in this second phase. It was concluded that specification is not related to group problem solving effectiveness and that group experience does not enhance individual problem solving.

Bibliography

Ammons, R. B., Ammons, C. H., and Morgan, R. L. Transfer of skill and decremental factors along the speed dimension in rotary pursuit. *Percept. Mot. Skills*, 1956, **6**, 43.

Andreas, B. G. *Experimental psychology*. New York: Wiley, 1960.

Arnoult, M. D. Transfer of predifferentiation training in simple and multiple shape discrimination. *J. exp. Psychol.*, 1953, **45**, 401–409.

Arnoult, M. D. Recognition of shapes following paired associates pretraining. In G. Finch and F. Cameron (Eds.), *Symposium on Air Force human engineering, personnel, and training research*. Washington: Nat. Acad. Sci.-Nat. Res. Council Publ. No. 455, 1956, pp. 1–9.

Arnoult, M. D. Stimulus predifferentiation: Some generalizations and hypotheses. *Psychol. Bull.*, 1957, **54**, 339–350.

Atkinson, R. C. (Ed.) *Studies in mathematical psychology*. Stanford, California: Stanford University Press, 1963.

Atwater, S. K. Proactive inhibition and associative facilitation as affected by degree of prior learning. *J. exp. Psychol.*, 1953, **46**, 400–405.

Barclay, A. Mediated transfer in verbal learning. *Psychol. Rep.*, 1963, **12**, 751–756.

Battig, W. F. Transfer from verbal pretraining to motor performance as a function of motor task complexity. *J. exp. Psychol.*, 1956, **51**, 371–378.

Bevan, W. Perceptual learning: an overview. *J. gen. Psychol.*, 1961, **64**, 69–99.

Bousfield, W. A. The occurrence of clustering in the recall of randomly arranged associates. *J. gen. Psychol.*, 1953, **49**, 229–240.

Bower, G. Application of a model to paired associate learning. *Psychometrika*, 1961, **26**, 255–280.

Bower, G. An association model for response and training variables in paired-associate learning. *Psychol. Rev.*, 1962, **69**, 34–53.

Bruce, R. W. Conditions of transfer of training. *J. exp. Psychol.*, 1933, **16**, 343–361.

Bruner, J. S., Mandler, J. M., O'Dowd, D., and Wallach, M. A. The role of overlearning and drive level in reversal learning. *J. comp. physiol. Psychol.*, 1958, **51**, 607–613.

Bugelski, B. R. Interferences with recall of original responses after learning new responses to old stimuli. *J. exp. Psychol.*, 1942, **30**, 368–379.

Bugelski, B. R. *The psychology of learning.* New York: Holt, Rinehart & Winston, 1956.

Bugelski, B. R., and Cadwallader, T. C. A reappraisal of the transfer and retroaction surface. *J. exp. Psychol.*, 1956, **52**, 360–366.

Bugelski, B. R., and Scharlock, D. P. An experimental demonstration of unconscious mediated association. *J. exp. Psychol.*, 1952, **44**, 334–338.

Bunch, M. E. The amount of transfer in rational learning as a function of time. *J. comp. Psychol.*, 1936, **22**, 325–337.

Bunch, M. E. Transfer of training in the mastery of an antagonistic habit after varying intervals of time. *J. comp. Psychol.*, 1939, **28**, 189–200.

Bunch, M. E. Cumulative transfer of training under different temporal conditions. *J. comp. Psychol.*, 1944, **37**, 265–272.

Bunch, M. E., and Lang, E. S. The amount of transfer of training from partial learning after varying intervals of time. *J. comp. Psychol.*, 1939, **27**, 449–459.

Bunch, M. E., and McCraven, V. Temporal course of transfer in the learning of memory material. *J. comp. Psychol.*, 1938, **25**, 481–496.

Bush, R. R., and Estes, W. K. (Eds.). *Studies in mathematical learning theory.* Stanford, California: Stanford University Press, 1959.

Buzzota, V. R. Association-probability in the study of verbal behavior. Unpublished doctoral dissertation, Washington University, 1956.

Cantor, G. N. Effects of three types of pretraining on discrimination learning in preschool children. *J. exp. Psychol.*, 1955, **49**, 339–342.

Campbell, V., and Freeman, J. T. Some functions of experimentally-induced language in perceptual learning. *Percept. mot. Skills*, 1955, **1**, 71–79.

Cheng, N. Y. Retroactive effect and degree of similarity. *J. exp. Psychol.*, 1929, **12**, 444–449.

Cofer, C. N., and Foley, J. P., Jr. Mediated generalization and the interpretation of verbal behavior: I. Prolegomena. *Psychol. Rev.*, 1942, **49**, 513–540.

Crafts, L. W. Routine and varying practice as preparation for adjustment to a new situation. *Arch. Psychol.*, N. Y., 1927, Vol. **14**, No. 91.

Crafts, L. W. Transfer as related to number of common elements. *J. gen. Psychol.*, 1935, **13**, 147–158.

Craig, R. C. *The transfer value of guided learning.* New York: Teachers College, Columbia University, 1953.

Crawford, J. L., and Vanderplas, J. M. An experiment on the mediation of transfer in paired-associate learning. *J. Psychol.*, 1959, **47**, 87–98.

Dallet, K. M. The transfer surface re-examined. *J. verb. Learn. verb. Behav.*, 1962, **1**, 91–94.

Dashiell, J. F. An experimental isolation of higher level habits. *J. exp. Psychol.*, 1924, **7**, 391–397.

Day, R. H. Relative task difficulty and transfer of training in skilled performance. *Psychol. Bull.*, 1956, **53**, 160–168.

Deese, J. *The psychology of learning.* New York: McGraw-Hill, 1958.

Dollard, J., and Miller, N. E. *Personality and psychotherapy.* New York: McGraw-Hill, 1950.

Dreis, T. A. Two studies in retroaction: I. Influence of partial identity. II. Susceptibility to retroaction at various grade levels. *J. gen. Psychol.*, 1933, **8**, 157–171.

Duncan, C. P. Transfer in motor learning as a function of degree of first-task learning and inter-task similarity. *J. exp. Psychol.*, 1953, **46**, 445–452.

Duncan, C. P. Transfer after training with single versus multiple tasks. *J. exp. Psychol.*, 1958, 1:**55**, 63–72.

Duncan, C. P. Recent research on human problem solving. *Psychol. Bull.*, 1959, **56**, 397–429.

Eckstrand, G. A., and Wickens, D. D. Transfer of perceptual set. *J. exp. Psychol.*, 1954, **47**, 274–278.

Ellis, H. C. Stimulus similarity and temporal factors in verbal transfer of training. Unpublished doctoral dissertation, Washington University, 1958.

Ellis, H. C. Judging the teaching effectiveness of programs. In G. D. Ofiesh and W. C. Meierhenry (Eds.), *Trends in Programmed Instruction.* Dept. of Audio-Visual Instruction, NEA and NSPI, 1964.

Ellis, H. C., Bessemer, D. W., Devine, J. V., and Trafton, C. L. Recognition of random tactual shapes following predifferentiation training. *Percept. Mot. Skills*, 1962, **10**, 99–102.

Ellis, H. C., and Burnstein, D. D. The effect of stimulus similarity and temporal factors in perceptual transfer of training. Technical Report No. 1, 1960, Sandia Corporation, Albuquerque, New Mexico.

Ellis, H. C., and Hunter, J. E. Response meaningfulness and the temporal course of transfer. Technical Report No. 2, 1960, Sandia Corporation, Albuquerque, New Mexico.

Ellis, H. C., and Hunter, J. E. The effect of response familiarization on the temporal course of transfer. Technical Report No. 3, 1961, Sandia Corporation, Albuquerque, New Mexico.

Ellis, H. C., and Hunter, J. E. A comparison of the temporal course of retention and non-specific transfer. Technical Report No. 4, 1961, Sandia Corporation, Albuquerque, New Mexico.

Ellis, H. C., and Muller, D. G. Transfer in perceptual learning following stimulus predifferentiation training. *J. exp. Psychol.*, 1964, **68**, 388–395.

Ehrenfreund, D. A study of the transposition gradient. *J. exp. Psychol.*, 1952, **43**, 83–87.

Estes, W. K. The statistical approach to learning theory. In S. Koch (Ed.), *Psychology: A study of a science*, **II**, 380–491. New York: McGraw-Hill, 1959.

Foley, J. P., Jr., and Cofer, C. N. Mediated generalization and the interpretation of verbal behavior: II. Experimental study of certain homophone and synonym gradients. *J. exp. Psychol.*, 1943, **32**, 168–175.

Gagné, R. M., Forster, H., and Crowley, M. E. The measurement of transfer of training. *Psychol. Bull.*, 1948, **45**, 97–130.

Gagné, R. M. The acquisition of knowledge. *Psychol. Rev.*, 1962, **69**, 355–365.

Gagné, R. M., and Baker, K. E. Stimulus predifferentiation as a factor in transfer of training. *J. exp. Psychol.*, 1950, **40**, 439–451.

Gagné, R. M., and Dick, W. Learning measures in a self-instructional program in solving equations. *Psychol. Rep.*, 1962, **10**, 131–146.

Gaier, E. L. The relationship between selected personality variables and the thinking of students in discussion classes. *Sch. Rev.*, 1952, **40**, 404–411.

Gibson, E. J. A systematic application of the concepts of generalization and differentiation to verbal learning. *Psychol. Rev.*, 1940, **47**, 196–229.

Gibson, E. J. Retroactive inhibition as a function of the degree of generalization between tasks. *J. exp. Psychol.*, 1941, **28**, 93–115.

Gibson, E. J. Perceptual learning. *Ann. Rev. Psychol.*, 1963, **14**, 29–56.

Gibson, J. J., and Gibson, E. J. Perceptual learning: differentiation or enrichment? *Psychol. Rev.*, 1955, **62**, 32–41.

Gladis, M. Grade differences in transfer as a function of the time interval between learning tasks. *J. educ. Psychol.*, 1960, **51**, 191–194.

Goldstein, D. A., and Newton, J. M. Transfer of training as a function of task difficulty in a complex control situation. *J exp. Psychol.*, 1962, **63**, 370–375.

Goss, A. E. Transfer as a function of type and amount of preliminary experience with the task stimuli. *J. exp. Psychol.*, 1953, **46**, 419–428.

Goss, A. E. A stimulus-response analysis of the interaction of cue-producing and mediating responses. *Psychol. Rev.*, 1955, **62**, 20–31.

Goss, A. E., and Greenfeld, N. Transfer to a motor task as influenced by conditions and degree of prior discrimination training. *J. exp. Psychol.*, 1958, 3:**55**, 258–269.

Greenspoon, J. The effects on transfer of time delay and task similarity:

A literature review. Technical Documentary Report No. AMRL–TDR–63–22, Wright-Patterson Air Force Base, Ohio, 1963.

Grice, G. R., and Saltz, E.   The generalization of an instrumental response to stimuli varying in the size dimension. *J. exp. Psychol.*, 1950, **40**, 702–708.

Gurnee, H.   Maze learning in the collective situation. *J. Psychol.*, 1937, **3**, 437–443.

Guttman, N.   Laws of behavior and facts of perception. In S. Koch (Ed.), *Psychology: A study of science*, V, 114–178. New York: McGraw-Hill, 1963.

Guttman, N., and Kalish, H. I.   Discriminability and stimulus generalization. *J. exp. Psychol.*, 1956, **51**, 79–88.

Haagen, C. H.   Learning and retention as a function of the synonymity of original and interpolated tasks. Unpublished doctoral dissertation, University of Iowa, 1943.

Haagen, C. H.   Synonymity, vividness, familiarity and association value ratings of 400 pairs of common adjectives. *J. Psychol.*, 1949, **27**, 453–463.

Hake, H. W., and Eriksen, C. W.   Effect of number of permissible response categories on learning of a constant number of visual stimuli. *J. exp. Psychol.*, 1955, **50**, 161–167.

Hake, H. W., and Ericksen, C. W.   Role of response variables in recognition and identification of complex visual forms. *J. exp. Psychol.*, 1956, **52**, 235–243.

Hamilton, C. E.   The relationship between length of interval separating two learning tasks and performance on the second task. *J. exp. Psychol.*, 1950, **40**, 613–621.

Hamilton, R. J.   Retroactive facilitation as a function of degree of generalization between tasks. *J. exp. Psychol.*, 1943, **32**, 363–376.

Harden, L. M.   A quantitative study of the similarity factor in retroactive inhibition. *J. gen. Psychol.*, 1929, **2**, 421–430.

Harlow, H. F.   The formation of learning sets. *Psychol. Rev.*, 1949, **56**, 51–65.

Harlow, H. F.   Thinking. In H. Helson (Ed.), *Theoretical foundations of psychology*, pp. 452–500. New York: Van Nostrand, 1951.

Harlow, H. F.   Learning set and error factor theory. In S. Koch (Ed.), *Psychology: A study of science*, 2, 492–537. New York: McGraw-Hill, 1959.

Heath, D.   Stimulus similarity and task familiarity as determinants of expectancy generalization. *J. exp. Psychol.*, 1959, **58**, 289–294.

Hendrickson, G., and Schroeder, W.   Transfer of training in learning to hit a submerged target. *J. educ. Psychol.*, 1941, **32**, 206–213.

Hilgard, E. R., Irvine, R. P., and Whipple, J. E.   Rote memorization, understanding, and transfer: An extension of Katona's card-trick experiments. *J. exp. Psychol.*, 1953, **46**, 288–292.

Holding, D. H. Transfer between difficult and easy tasks. *Brit. J. Psychol.*, 1962, **53**, 397–407.

Hovland, C. I. The generalization of conditioned responses with varying frequencies of tone. *J. gen. Psychol.*, 1937, **17**, 125–148.

Hovland, C. I., and Kurtz, K. H. Experimental studies in rote-learning theory: X. Pre-learning syllable familiarization and the length-difficulty relationship. *J. exp. Psychol.*, 1952, **44**, 31–39.

Hudgins, B. B. Effects of group experience on individual problem solving. *J. educ. Psychol.*, 1960, Vol. **51**, No. 1, pp. 37–42.

Hull, C. L. Goal attraction and directing ideas conceived as habit phenomena. *Psychol. Rev.*, 1931, **38**, 487–506.

Hull, C. L. *Principles of behavior.* New York: Appleton-Century-Crofts, 1943.

Jenkins, J. J., and Russell, W. A. Associative clustering during recall. *J. abnorm. soc. Psychol.*, 1952, **47**, 818–821.

Johnson, L. M. Similarity of meaning as a factor in retroactive inhibition. *J. gen. Psychol.*, 1933, **9**, 377–388.

Judd, C. H. The relation of special training and general intelligence. *Educ. Rev.*, 1908, **36**, 42–48.

Jung, J. Effects of response meaningfulness (m) on transfer under two different paradigms. *J. exp. Psychol.*, 1963, **65**, 377–384.

Kelley, H. H., and Thibaut, J. W. Experimental studies of group problem solving and process. In G. Lindzey (Ed.), *Handbook of social psychology.* Vol. **2**, *Special fields and applications*, pp. 735–785. Cambridge, Massachusetts: Addison-Wesley, 1954.

Kendler, T. S. An experimental investigation of transposition as a function of the difference between training and test stimuli. *J. exp. Psychol.*, 1950, **40**, 552–562.

Kennelly, T. W. The role of similarity in retroactive inhibition. *Arch. Psychol.*, N. Y., 1941, Vol. **37**, No. 260.

Kent, G. H., and Rosanoff, A. J. A study of association in insanity. *Amer. J. Insanity*, 1910, **67**, 37–96, 317–390.

Kingsley, H. L., and Garry, R. *The nature and conditions of learning.* (2nd ed.) Englewood Cliffs, New Jersey: Prentice-Hall, 1957.

Klugman, S. F. Cooperative versus individual efficiency in problem solving. *J. educ. Psychol.*, 1944, **35**, 91–100.

Kohler, W. *The mentality of apes.* New York: Harcourt, Brace, & World, 1925.

Kuenne, M. R. Experimental investigation of the relation of language to transposition behavior in young children. *J. exp. Psychol.*, 1946, **36**, 471–490.

Lawrence, D. H.   The transfer of a discrimination along a continuum. *J. comp. physiol. Psychol.*, 1952, **45**, 511–516.

Lifton, H., and Goss, A. E.   Aural-visual transfer of paired-associates learning. *J. gen. Psychol.*, 1962, **66**, 225–234.

Lordahl, D. S., and Archer, E. J.   Transfer effects on a rotary pursuit task as a function of first-task difficulty. *J. exp. Psychol.*, 1958, **56**, 421–426.

Lorge, I., Fox, D., Davitz J., and Brenner, M.   A survey of studies contrasting the quality of group performance and individual performance, 1920–1957. *Psychol. Bull.*, 1958, **55**, 337–372.

Lumsdaine, A. A., and Glaser, R.   *Teaching machines and programmed learning*. Washington, D.C. National Education Association, 1960.

Maltzman, I.   Thinking: From a behavioristic viewpoint. *Psychol. Rev.*, 1955, **62**, 275–286.

Mandler, G.   From association to structure. *Psychol. Rev.*, 1962, **69**, 415–427.

Mandler, G., and Heinemann, S. H.   Effect of overlearning of a verbal response on transfer of training. *J. exp. Psychol.*, 1956, **51**, 39–46.

Marx, M. H.   The effects of cumulative training upon retroactive inhibition and transfer. *Comp. Ps. Monogr.*, No. 94, 1944.

Marx, M. H.   Some suggestions for the conceptual and theoretical analysis of complex intervening variables in problem-solving behavior. *J. gen. Psychol.*, 1958, **58**, 115–128.

McAllister, D. E.   The effects of various kinds of relevant verbal pretraining on subsequent motor performance. *J. exp. Psychol.*, 1953, **46**, 329–336.

McGeoch, J. A.   *The psychology of human learning*. New York: Longmans, Green, 1942.

McGeoch, J. A., and Irion, A. L.   *The psychology of human learning*. Second edition. New York: Longmans, Green, 1952.

McGeoch, J. A., and McDonald, W. T.   Meaningful relation and retroactive inhibition. *Amer. J. Psychol.*, 1931, 579–588.

McGeoch, J. A., and McGeoch, G. O.   Studies in retroactive inhibition: X. The influence of similarity of meaning between lists of paired associates. *J. exp. Psychol.*, 1937, **21**, 320–329.

McKinney, F.   Quantitative and qualitative essential elements of transfer. *J. exp. Psychol.*, 1933, **16**, 854–864.

Melton, A. W.   The methodology of experimental studies of human learning and retention: I. The functions of a methodology and the available criteria for evaluating different experimental methods. *Psychol. Bull.*, 1936, **33**, 305–394.

Melton, A. W.   Materials for use in experimental studies of the learning and retention of verbal habits. Unpublished manuscript, University of Missouri, 1940.

Melton, A. W. The science of learning and the technology of educational methods. *Harvard Educ. Rev.*, 1959, **29**, 96–106.

Melton, A. W. (Ed.). *Categories of human learning.* New York: Academic Press, 1964.

Melton, A. W., and Von Lackum, W. J. Retroactive and proactive inhibition in retention: Evidence for a two-factor theory of retroactive inhibition. *Amer. J. Psychol.*, 1941, **54**, 157–173.

Miller, G. A. *Language and communication.* New York: McGraw-Hill, 1951.

Miller, N. E., and Dollard, J. *Social learning and imitation.* New Haven: Yale University Press, 1941.

Morgan, R. L., and Underwood, B. J. Proactive inhibition as a function of response similarity. *J. exp. Psychol.*, 1950, **40**, 592–603.

Morrisett, L. J., and Hovland, C. I. A comparison of three varieties of training in human problem solving. *J. exp. Psychol.*, 1959, **58**, 52–55.

Murdock, B. B., Jr. Transfer designs and formulas. *Psychol. Bull.*, 1957, **54**, 313–326.

Namikas, G., and Archer, E. J. Motor skill transfer as a function of intertask interval and pretransfer task difficulty. *J. exp. Psychol.*, 1960, **59**, 109–112.

Noble, C. E. Meaningfulness (*m*) and transfer phenomena in serial verbal learning. Paper presented at the 31st meeting of the Midwestern Psychological Association, Chicago, 1959.

Norcross, K. J., and Spiker, C. C. Effects of mediated association on transfer in paired-associate learning. *J. exp. Psychol.*, 1958, **55**, 129–134.

Osgood, C. E. Meaningful similarity and interference in learning. *J. exp. Psychol.*, 1946, **36**, 244–301.

Osgood, C. E. An investigation into the causes of retroactive interference. *J. exp. Psychol.*, 1948, **38**, 132–154.

Osgood, C. E. The similarity paradox in human learning: A resolution. *Psychol. Rev.*, 1949, **56**, 132–143.

Osgood, C. E. *Method and theory in experimental psychology.* New York: Oxford, 1953.

Palermo, D. S. Mediated association in a paired-associate transfer task. *J. exp. Psychol.*, 1962, **64**, 234–238.

Perlmutter, H. V., and de Montmollin, G. Group learning of nonsense syllables. *J. abnorm. soc. Psychol.*, 1952, **47**, 762–769.

Peters, H. N. Mediate association. *J. exp. Psychol.*, 1935, **18**, 20–48.

Pond, F. L.   Influence of the study of Latin on word knowledge. *School Rev.*, 1938, **46**, 611–618.

Porter, L. W., and Duncan, C. P.   Negative transfer in verbal learning. *J. exp. Psychol.*, 1953, **46**, 61–64.

Postman, L.   Association theory and perceptual learning. *Psychol. Rev.*, 1955, **62**, 438–446.

Postman, L.   Transfer of training as a function of experimental paradigm and degree of first-list learning. *J. verbal Learn. verbal Behav.*, 1962, **1**, 109–118.

Postman, L.   Perception and learning. In S. Koch (Ed.), *Psychology: A study of science*, V, 30–113. New York: McGraw-Hill, 1963.

Reid, L. S.   The development of noncontinuity behavior through continuity learning. *J. exp. Psychol.*, 1953, **46**, 107–112.

Rickert, E. J.   Application of Bower's association model to paired-associate transfer. Unpublished master's thesis, University of New Mexico, 1963.

Riley, D. A.   The nature of the effective stimulus in animal discrimination learning: Transposition reconsidered. *Psychol. Rev.*, 1958, **65**, 1–7.

Riopelle, A. J.   Transfer suppression and learning sets. *J. comp. physiol. Psychol.*, 1953, **46**, 61–64.

Robinson, E. S.   The "similarity" factor in retroaction. *Amer. J. Psychol.*, 1927, **39**, 297–312.

Robinson, J. S.   The effect of learning labels for stimuli on their later discrimination. *J. exp. Psychol.*, 1955, **49**, 112–115.

Rothkopf, E. Z.   A measure of stimulus similarity and errors in some paired-associate learning tasks. *J. exp. Psychol.*, 1957, **53**, 94–101.

Rudel, R. G.   Transposition of response to size in children. *J. comp. physiol. Psychol.*, 1958, **51**, 386–390.

Russell, W. A., and Storms, L. H.   Implicit verbal chaining in paired-associate learning. *J. exp. Psychol.*, 1955, **49**, 287–293.

Schulz, R. W.   Problem solving behavior and transfer. *Harvard Educ. Rev.*, 1960, **30**, 61–77.

Siipola, E. M., and Israel, H. E.   Habit interference as dependent upon stage of training. *Amer. J. Psychol.*, 1933, **45**, 205–227.

Siipola, E. M.   The relation of transfer to similarity in habit-structure. *J. exp. Psychol.*, 1941, **28**, 233–261.

Skinner, B. F.   The science of learning and the art of teaching. *Harvard Educ. Rev.*, 1954, **24**, 86–97.

Skinner, B. F.   Teaching machines. *Science*, 1958, **128**, 969–977.

Spence, K. W.   The differential response in animals to stimuli varying within a single dimension. *Psychol. Rev.*, 1937, **44**, 430–444.

Spence, K. W. *Behavior theory and conditioning.* New Haven: Yale University Press, 1956.

Spence, K. W. The relation of learning theory to the technology of education. *Harvard Educ. Rev.*, 1959, **29**, 84–95.

Spence, K. W. Anxiety (Drive) level and performance in eyelid conditioning. *Psychol. Bull.*, 1964, **61**, 129–139.

Stolurow, L. M. *Teaching by machine.* Cooperative Research Monograph No. 6. Washington, D.C., U.S. Government Printing Office, 1961.

Stolurow, L. M. Comparative studies of principles for programming mathematics in automated instruction. Semi-Annual Report, Educational Media Branch, U.S. Office of Education, Project No. 711/51.01, 1963.

Taber, J. I., and Glaser, R. An exploratory evaluation of a discriminative transfer learning program using literal prompts. *J. educ. Res.*, 1962, **55**, 508–512.

Taylor, D. W., and Faust, W. L. Twenty questions: Efficiency in problem solving as a function of size of group. *J. exp. Psychol.*, 1952, **44**, 360–368.

Thorndike, E. L., and Woodworth, R. S. The influence of improvement in one mental function upon the efficiency of other functions. (I); II. The estimation of magnitudes; III. Functions involving attention, observation and discrimination. *Psychol. Rev.*, 1901, **8**, 247–261, 384–395, 553–564.

Thorndike, E. L., and Lorge, I. *The teacher's word book of 30,000 words.* New York: Teachers College, Columbia University, 1944.

Thune, L. E. The effect of different types of preliminary activities on subsequent learning of paired-associate material. *J. exp. Psychol.*, 1950, **40**, 423–438.

Tolman, E. C. *Purposive behavior in animals and men.* New York: Appleton-Century-Crofts, 1932.

Twedt, H. M., and Underwood, B. J. Mixed vs. unmixed lists in transfer studies. *J. exp. Psychol.*, 1959, **58**, 111–116.

Underwood, B. J. The effect of successive interpolations on retroactive and proactive inhibition. *Psychol. Monogr.*, 1945, **59**, No. 273.

Underwood, B. J. *Experimental psychology; an introduction.* New York: Appleton-Century-Crofts, 1949. (a)

Underwood, B. J. Proactive inhibition as a function of time and degree of prior learning. *J. exp. Psychol.*, 1949, **39**, 24–34. (b)

Underwood, B. J. Associative transfer in verbal learning as a function of response similarity and degree of first-list learning. *J. exp. Psychol.*, 1951, **42**, 44–54.

Underwood, B. J. *Psychological research*. New York: Appleton-Century-Crofts, 1957.

Underwood, B. J. Verbal learning in the educative process. *Harvard Educ. Rev.*, 1959, **29**, 107–117.

Underwood, B. J. An evaluation of the Gibson theory of verbal learning. In C. N. Cofer (Ed.), *Verbal learning and verbal behavior*, pp. 197–217. New York: McGraw-Hill, 1961.

Underwood, B. J., and Hughes, R. H. Gradients of generalized verbal responses. *Amer. J. Psychol.*, 1950, **63**, 422–430.

Underwood, B. J., Runquist, W. R., and Schulz, R. W. Response learning in paired-associate lists as a function of intra-list similarity. *J. exp. Psychol.*, 1959, **58**, 70–78.

Underwood, B. J., and Schulz, R. W. *Meaningfulness and verbal learning*. Chicago: Lippincott, 1960.

Vanderplas, J. M. Transfer of training and its relation to perceptual learning and recognition. *Psychol. Rev.*, 1958, **65**, 375–385.

Vanderplas, J. M. Associative processes and task relations in perceptual learning. *Percept. Mot. Skills*, 1963, **16**, 501–509.

Vanderplas, J. M., Sanderson, W. A., and Vanderplas, J. N. Some task-related determinants of transfer in perceptual learning. *Percept. Mot. Skills*, 1964, **18**, 71–80.

Vanderplas, J. M., and Garvin, E. A. Complexity, association value, and practice as factors in shape recognition following paired-associates training. *J. exp. Psychol.*, 1959, **57**, 155–163.

Ward, L. B. Reminiscence and rote learning. *Psychol. Monogr.*, 1937, Vol. **49**, No. 220.

Watson, B. The similarity factor in transfer and inhibition. *J. educ. Psychol.*, 1938, **29**, 145–157.

Werner, O. H. The influence of the study of modern foreign language on the development of desirable abilities in English. *Stud. in mod. Lang. Teach.*, 1930, **17**, 97–145.

Wickens, D. D. The transference of conditioned excitation and conditioned inhibition from one muscle group to the antagonistic muscle group. *J. exp. Psychol.*, 1938, **22**, 101–123.

Wohlwill, J. F. The learning of absolute and relational number discriminations by children. *J. genet. Psychol.*, 1962, **101**, 217–228.

Woodrow, H. The effect of training upon transference. *J. educ. Psychol.* 1927, **18**, 159–172.

Woodworth, R. S. *Experimental psychology*. New York: Holt, Rinehart & Winston, 1938.

Woodworth, R. S., and Schlosberg, H. *Experimental psychology*. Revised edition. New York: Holt, Rinehart & Winston, 1954.

Wylie, H. H. An experimental study of transfer of response in the white rat. *Behav. Monogr.*, 1919, Vol. 3, No. 16.

Young, R. K., and Underwood, B. J. Transfer in verbal materials with dissimilar stimuli and response similarity varied. *J. exp. Psychol.*, 1954, 47, 153–159.

Yum, K. W. An experimental test of the law of assimilation. *J. exp. Psychol.*, 1931, 14, 68–82.

Index